PARANORMAL EXPERIENCES

PARANORMAL EXPERIENCES

AS TOLD BY A GETTYSBURG GHOST TOUR GUIDE

D.E. POPE

PARANORMAL EXPERIENCES
AS TOLD BY A GETTYSBURG GHOST TOUR GUIDE

Interior Image Credit: Shane Moran
Editor: David Bailey

iUniverse books may be ordered through booksellers or by contacting:

iUniverse
1663 Liberty Drive
Bloomington, IN 47403
www.iuniverse.com
844-349-9409

ISBN: 978-1-6632-3697-5 (sc)
ISBN: 978-1-6632-3877-1 (e)

Library of Congress Control Number: 2022907513

Print information available on the last page.

iUniverse rev. date: 04/28/2022

A SPECIAL THANK YOU TO
TIFFANY LANDRY FOR ALL OF THE
BEHIND THE SCENES HELP.

IN MEMORY OF MOM AND DAD,
WHOSE SUPPORT NEVER WAVERED.

INTRODUCTION

"Who are you? Why are you here? I think I know why . . . you came to seek me out, to blame me for a crime that I never committed!" I bellowed this at the start of every Johnny Reb Ghostly Encounter tour. Who exactly is Johnny Reb? You will find out in these pages, but a word to the wise: Do not forget his name!

It all began in the late winter of 2010 when I saw a help-wanted ad in a local newspaper. I was not looking for a job, but when I saw the job title, "Ghost Tour Guides Wanted," I thought I would check it out.

I soon found out that the job was focused on two of the most haunted areas in Gettysburg, Pennsylvania: The Jennie Wade House and the Soldiers National Museum, also known as the Orphanage. Having grown up in the area, I knew all about the amazing history of this once quaint, peaceful town, now a lively, bustling community that thrives on tourism. Tourism fueled in part because Gettysburg was (and still is) considered one of the most haunted small towns in America.

Jennie Wade House

Soldiers National
Museum a.k.a.
Orphanage

Why is Gettysburg so haunted?" I was often asked this question, and my answer was always the same, "I'm no expert, but being the home of the bloodiest battle ever fought on American soil may have something to do with it."

After answering the help-wanted ad, going through three extremely nerve-wracking auditions, and extensive training, I was a full-fledged ghost tour guide for, in my opinion, the best ghost tour company in Gettysburg.

As a tour guide, my objective was not to take away from the town's history. Instead, I wanted to offer guests of Gettysburg something they could entertain themselves with once the sun went down and the national park closed. Gettysburg was, is, and always will be known for the tragic events that occurred from July 1st to the 3rd in 1863; events that changed the course of history. But there will always be room for some evening entertainment that only the ghosts of Gettysburg can provide.

Five years, approximately one thousand tours, and several appearances on local television and syndicated ghost hunting shows later, my run had come to an end. Over the course of those five years, I was blessed to meet tens of thousands of thrill seekers and became friends with many of them. Many of these people made it a point to come back year after year, from as far away as Canada and California, to take one or more of my tours. They didn't care if they had already been on that particular tour, they were ready to go again. What I found so amazing was that our friendships did not stop when they left Gettysburg. Even during the company's "off-season" I would maintain contact with them, even attending their children's school musicals, orchestra concerts, and sporting events. These guests were truly loyal to me, and I tried to return the favor as much as possible.

During my incredible run, the ghost tours even provided a romantic interest, which produced a three-year relationship and some of the most memorable times of my life.

However, I would be lying if I said the tours were all good times. There were guests that absolutely loathed me. They would say I was loud, obnoxious, over-the-top, or downright unentertaining. While I hated to hear about those unhappy guests, I realized it was impossible to make every guest happy, so I took the good with the bad. Fortunately for me, the good far outweighed the bad.

I conducted just about every tour our company had to offer: walking tours, haunted bus tours, campfire tours, ghostly encounter tours, the Truth or Scare tours, the canine-companion tours (one of my favorites), and many more. It was not unusual to find me at one of the local campgrounds, entertaining campers on a ghost walk as a representative of the ghost tour company. Along with the tours, I had the opportunity to sit in on investigations conducted by some of the most renowned investigative teams in the country, and the world.

Along with the tours and investigations, I was fortunate enough to be interviewed by some of the paranormal television shows and given the opportunity to reflect on some of my favorite experiences, and believe me, there were many! On more than one occasion I was also asked to be a guest speaker to help raise money for charity. These were some of the proudest experiences I had as a ghost tour guide.

Why was I successful? I believe it had a lot to do with my mindset. I never felt like telling ghost stories was a job; instead, it was my passion. I did not like sharing ghost stories—I loved it! During my initial training session, I vividly recall the manager telling me that while I may do these tours every night, sometimes multiple times a night, it was all brand new to that guest in the crowd. I yearned to be the highlight of their vacation to Gettysburg and the reason they wanted to come back year after year. It was my goal to make the experience as memorable as possible, and I wholeheartedly believe I did a good job of that. Throughout the years, I was amazed at how many people spent their hard-earned money just to see and hear me talk about ghosts, and took enjoyment and satisfaction from that.

⸻◆⸻

Growing up within ten minutes of Gettysburg meant I was a frequent visitor. It was not unusual for my mom, dad, brother and myself to hop in the car on a Sunday afternoon and just drive around the battlefield. We would stop long enough for my brother and I to scale the rocks at Devils Den or walk up the narrow stone stairs to the top of the Pennsylvania Monument.

In addition to the Sunday afternoon drives with the family, it seemed like every other year my class would take a field trip to Gettysburg.

Incredibly, I never got bored with it. I loved the small town of about seven thousand residents, and was captivated by a place, only a few minutes from where I lived, that was such an important part of American history. While the loss of life was catastrophic, the fact of the matter remained that without the events that happened in early July, 1863, our great country would not be as it appears today.

My love for the town has never wavered. It even increased once my daughter was born. Although she was not a big fan of going on the ghost tours (she was scared of her own shadow), she was a fan of the town itself. I will always treasure the time we spent together walking the fields that possessed so much heritage. On any typical Saturday or Sunday, we, along with a friend of hers, could be found walking around the monuments, towers, and other important areas of the battlefield. It is my sincere hope that my beautiful daughter has as fond memories as I do of our time spent together in Gettysburg.

So, if I loved it so much, why did I retire after just five years? The answer is simple: exhaustion. There were times during that five-year stretch, especially during the dog-days of summer, where I would send myself into a total state of exhaustion. I had a full-time job from six in the morning until three in the afternoon, so it was not unusual for me to go home, rest for an hour or so, then head right up to Gettysburg to do my tours. If I did two tours a night, I would get back home at one or two in the morning, sleep for a few hours, and start the process all over again.

One memory of extreme exhaustion that really sticks out in my mind happened in the spring of 2012 where, between my full-time job and the ghost tours, I worked for twenty-six hours straight. By the end of the last tour, I was relying on pure adrenaline. While it was a blast, I paid a price for the lack of rest and sleep. I wasn't twenty years old anymore, I was in my forties. The thought of simply cutting back on my tours and investigations did cross my mind numerous times, but I was not that type of person. I went full speed ahead all the time, and anything less would have been a letdown.

Reminiscing, there were two questions that, if I had a dollar for every time they were asked, I would now be a multi-millionaire. The first question was "What was the strangest experience I have ever had conducting a tour or an investigation?" The answer to that question was always the same: there were so many it is impossible to rank in order. In the following chapters, I share some of the most memorable experiences during my tours. Some of these experiences are generated by my own perspectives, while others are from the perspectives of the most loyal guests a tour guide could ever ask for.

The second question was "Do you believe in ghosts?" I can say without a doubt, YES, I believe. If I was not a believer prior to conducting the ghost tours, more than enough happened to me that would have changed my mind. But I was a believer, and it started for me when I was only twelve years old. It was a beautiful, late August morning, and it happened on East Confederate Avenue.

CHAPTER 1

DID YOU SEE THAT?

My brother had turned sixteen, and he was so proud of his little silver Chevy Chevette. It was his first car, and after a couple attempts, he finally earned his driver's license. (I always loved rubbing it in to my brother that I was able to pass my driver's test during my first try.) Years later I would also own a Chevette, as my father believed that, due to its small size and nonpowerful engine, it was the perfect first car for both of his sons to begin the driving portions of their lives.

I was twelve when my brother got his car and still somewhat leery about riding in a car he was driving. As we approached the end of the summer vacation from school, he was able to talk me into going for a ride through the battlefield. My parents were both at work, and to celebrate our final few days of freedom, we hopped into his silver Chevette with the black-and-white checkered seats and headed toward Gettysburg.

It was my parents' rule that, during the final week of summer break, my brother and I would have to go to bed at our normal school night time so we could get acclimated to the upcoming school year. My bedtime was 8:30 and his was 9:30, so we were well rested and awoke early on that late August morning.

After a near-death experience of him turning in front of a tractor trailer (he always points out with a smile the truck would have hit my side first), we entered the hallowed grounds of the battlefield via Confederate Avenue. It was still early, well before ten in the morning, and the area was as quiet and serene as an ancient landscape unspoiled by the twenty-first century.

Within a half mile of turning onto Confederate Avenue, I spotted a man emerging from the woods, and heading toward the road my brother and I were traveling.

At twelve years old, and growing up in and around Gettysburg, I knew the difference between the Union and Confederate soldiers. Because of what the man was wearing, I immediately identified him as portraying a Confederate soldier. Between his gray pants, dilapidated white shirt, and no shoes, he looked amazingly authentic, and because of the rifle he was carrying, and the canteen around his neck, I assumed he was a member of a re-enactment group.

I watched in awe as the unknown man reached the road, turned, and began walking toward us. I was waiting for the reenactor to raise his hand and acknowledge my brother and I, but to my chagrin it never happened. As we slowly passed him, he continued to simply stare ahead, like he was on some sort of mission. A little put off by the fact he failed to even look our way, I immediately turned as we passed him to grab one final look. I was in utter shock when I realized the anti-social man was nowhere to be found. Turning my head in every direction, I frantically looked for him, but he was gone. He simply vanished.

To this day, when I tell people about this experience, they offer one of two explanations. The first is I was dreaming and/or hallucinating. If that was truly the case, I supposed my brother was having the same dream and/or hallucination, because he witnessed the same thing I did.

The second explanation is that the reenactor simply walked back into the woods after we drove by him. The timing with this explanation makes it impossible. I did not wait five or ten seconds to turn and look at the man. I immediately turned around once we had passed him, and he was not there. What I do know is that the man was there one moment and gone the next. Of course, being the junior investigators my brother and I were, we quickly circled the area looking for the man, but he was gone.

What did we see that day? Was it a spirit? What exactly is a spirit? According to the *Webster's New World Dictionary and Thesaurus*, Second Edition, the word *spirit* is defined as "a supernatural being, as a ghost or angel." I believe spirits are stuck between this world and the afterlife. They suffered sudden and tragic loss of life.

To better relate this definition to what I saw that day, picture a young man in his mid-to-late teens who is away from his family for the first time in his short life. He is fighting for his and his family's beliefs in the bloodiest battle ever fought on American soil. Perhaps he was standing atop the rocks at Devils Den, or attacking at Big Round Top, or filling his canteen down by Spangler Spring, or even charging the Union soldiers as part of General George Pickett's division on the third and final day of the battle. Suddenly, he is shot and killed, taken from his family and his loved ones before his life really began. It does not get much more sudden and tragic than that.

So, what really did I see that day? I am absolutely convinced I saw the spirit of a young Confederate soldier, meandering around the battlefield, perhaps close to where he lost his life. During my days as a ghost tour guide, I encountered three different types of guests: those who will take to their graves their belief there is no such thing as a ghost, those who are undecided, and those who wholeheartedly believe ghosts exist. After witnessing what I saw on that early August morning, I definitely fall into that third category. I sincerely believe ghosts and spirits exist, that they are abundant in and around Gettysburg, and that I witnessed one up close and personal. For me, seeing WAS believing.

That experience happened decades before I became a ghost tour guide, but it is where my fascination for the paranormal began. It was my first experience, but definitely not my last.

CHAPTER 2

WHO IS AT THE DOOR?

To most the visitors to Gettysburg, it is hard to believe the town existed prior to the first shots fired during the battle. As you stroll through the town, you cannot help but take notice of the many bronze "Civil War Building, July 1863" signs hanging on existing dwellings. Throughout this book, I will mention several buildings and landmarks which did exist prior to and during the three-day battle.

One such building that played a pivotal role in the battle sits several miles west of town and is known as the Cashtown Inn. The purpose of the inn, built in 1797, was to provide lodging, food, and drink to travelers on the Gettysburg-Chambersburg Turnpike. The innkeeper only accepted cash as payment for services, therefore, the building, and the surrounding area, became known as Cashtown.

In late June 1863, Confederate General A.P. Hill arrived at the inn and used it as his headquarters during the upcoming battle. There was constant foot-traffic of Confederate soldiers going in and out of the inn before, during, and after the battle, and many people believe that, to this day, the action has never ended.

Even though the Cashtown Inn was not one of the buildings I had the opportunity to investigate and conduct tours through, it always seemed to be a topic of conversation between my guests and me.

One of the many things I loved about being a tour guide was the fellowship I enjoyed with the people who went on my tours. They were anxious to hear about my experiences, but they also enjoyed sharing their own.

One of the stories they shared with me involving the inn were about the swing that occupied the front porch. It was not unusual on a hot, steamy night, with little to no wind whatsoever, to see the it start swinging back and forth with no one visible sitting in it.

At the inn, footsteps could be heard running through the hallways; lights were seen flickering on and off throughout the building; strange, unexplained noises, such as men's cries, were often detected in the guest rooms; and the list goes on and on.

A good friend of my father was often a frequent guest of the inn, along with his wife. He had a heart condition and was therefore on some potent medication. Along with being strong, the medicine was quite pricey, so because of its life-saving effectiveness, and the expenses associated with it, he was always cognizant of where this particular medication was. Every evening, as a nightly routine, he would always pull out his medication for the next day and place it on his nightstand so he would know where it was the following morning. Following protocol, during one of his stays at the inn, he did just that. The next morning when he went to take his pills, he quickly realized the medication he had sat out the night before was not on the nightstand. He asked his wife where she moved his pills to, and she was dumbfounded. Despite getting down on their hands and knees, and looking all over the floor, including underneath the bed and nightstand, his pills were nowhere to be found. Up to this day if you ask him what happened to his medication that night, he will tell you that someone or something took it, and it was not one of them.

As previously mentioned, the Cashtown Inn was a constant source of discussion during and after my tours. After a tour one evening, Debbie and Mark L., from Hartford, Connecticut, shared an experience they had while staying at the inn. Before coming to Gettysburg and staying at the Cashtown Inn, they had watched an episode of one of the prominent ghost hunting shows on television. The episode they watched focused on the inn, and ultimately prompted them into staying in Cashtown.

Mark and Debbie were not only ghost enthusiasts, they were also history buffs interested in the Civil War, so staying at the Cashtown Inn was a no-brainer for them. When they arrived at the destination, they were thrilled when they were told they had the General Robert E. Lee suite (Room 5).

Having arrived late in the day, they decided to simply relax after their nearly six-hour drive. They unpacked, enjoyed dinner in the inn's dining room, and followed that up with a nice, leisurely sunset drive around the battlefield.

After their uneventful drive, they decided to retire early to their room. Anxious for the adventures that laid ahead of them, but exhausted from driving all day, they turned the lights out and went to bed. It did not take long for unexplained events to occur.

At some point in the middle of the night, they both were awakened by a noise that to them sounded like someone jiggling their doorknob, as if they were trying to get into their guestroom. Mark quickly checked the door and found nothing. Certain that they had heard something, they had trouble falling back to sleep. Eventually they did, but then Debbie was awoken to the same noise she had heard previously. Checking her watch on the nightstand, she noticed it was quarter after four in the morning. Still hearing the noise after several minutes, she nudged Mark awake, and they both listened once again. The noise eventually stopped, but sleep at that point was impossible, so the couple watched some early morning television before embarking on the activities of the day.

"What was it?" they asked me after my tour. Of course, I did not have an answer. It could have been someone trying to break into their room, but my guess is it was one of the thousands and thousands of Confederate soldiers who lost their lives during the battle. Regardless of the actual answer, which will never be known, it brought back a memory of a personal experience I had encountered at the Inn approximately one decade before.

Long before my days of being a ghost tour guide, my wife (now ex) and I decided to spend a few days at the fabled Inn. It was the middle of November, about a week or so before Thanksgiving, and we made the short drive to Cashtown. After checking into the General Robert E. Lee suite Monday afternoon, we had a delicious dinner that was fit for a king and queen.

After dinner, we returned to our room, and I watched the Monday night football game on the television. My wife, who was not into football, began reading some of the journal entries that were left in the guest logbook located on the counter. The journal entries were so interesting, she was able to coax me into reading some of the written experiences.

Having been well versed, even at that time, with the paranormal history in Gettysburg, including the Cashtown Inn, I was admittedly a little nervous about what the night may bring. Reading some of the stories did not help ease my apprehensiveness either. After the football game had ended, my wife and I couldn't fall asleep, so we simply laid in bed talking to each other. We did hear some noises in the room, but we quickly chalked that up to being the product of an extremely old building cracking and settling, and the gusty wind blowing outside.

At that time, I owned my own business, so the following morning, after getting very little sleep, I had to make a quick appearance at work for a few hours. Instead of being able to get some work done, however, the Inn dominated my thoughts. I researched the Cashtown Inn on the internet, and after a couple hours, returned to join my wife, armed with a lot more knowledge than I had the night before, especially the haunted history of the building. And we all know the saying, "a little bit of knowledge can be dangerous."

For the rest of the afternoon and evening, which included another delicious prime rib dinner in the dining room, I was a nervous wreck. Everywhere I went I was looking over my shoulder. Every time I heard a noise, I would jerk my head and look around, my paranoia growing as the evening went on. I had made the decision earlier in the day that I was not going to read any more of the journal entries, but as I sat down to relax, I found myself drawn to them. Reading one experience after another, my anxiety intensified, especially after my wife and I decided to turn in for the evening.

Falling asleep was definitely not easy, and I am not sure when I eventually did, but it happened. Neither of us slept very well, and after every bump in the night we would ask each other, "Did you hear that?" On several different occasions I jumped out of bed, quickly turned on the lights, and inspected the suite. After not finding anything out of the ordinary, I would hesitantly crawl back in bed, pondering the journal entries I had read just hours before. Normally I have no trouble falling asleep, but on this cold night in the middle of November, I found sleep impossible, and was busy wishing the night away.

My anxiety came to a head when I heard what sounded like someone attempting to enter our room. The doorknob rattled and seconds later

I heard footsteps just outside, walking away from our door. Almost immediately I again heard footsteps, this time getting louder and louder, followed by another rattling of the doorknob. My wife, whom I believed was asleep during all of this, asked, "What time is it?". Having no idea, I jumped out of bed, turned the light on, and noticed that clock read five. Of course, I looked to see who was at our door, but nobody was there. Everything seemed quiet, at least on our floor.

Determined to stay awake in case the doorknob rattled again, I laid in bed until daylight, at which time I got up and watched the morning news, allowing my wife to get some more sleep. When she did eventually awaken, she surprised me when she asked, "Who was trying to get into our room in the middle of the night?"

Tired and weary, I made my way downstairs and sought out one of the owners. My first question to her was, "Who could have been trying to get into our room at five in the morning?" With a sympathetic look in her eyes, she informed me that my wife and I were the only human beings in the inn the previous night. There were no other guests, and the entire staff had gone home, which was not unusual for that time of year.

Since that night, I have been told time and time again that the occurrence was simply our imaginations. The inn's owner may have been correct, that my wife and I were the only living inhabitants in the building, but I truly believe we were sharing the Inn with someone or something not of this world.

I will never forget our stay at the Cashtown Inn. The beautiful, peaceful, and elegant pre–Civil War structure provided me with a taste of a truly haunted building. Little did I know at the time that in less than a decade, I would start my ghost tour career in one of the most haunted buildings in the United States.

CHAPTER 3

YOU HAVE OUR ATTENTION

The very first ghost tour I conducted in 2010 was inside a small brick building known as the Jennie Wade House. This is also where I spent a majority of my time during my five-year tenure. The accolades for this renowned building are endless, including being named one of the scariest haunted houses in America by CBS News (Scariest haunted houses in U.S; October 28, 2010), as well as being recognized as one of the top ten scariest places in America by the Travel Channel. The home has also been featured on many of the paranormal shows on television.

Like the Cashtown Inn, the Jennie Wade house was erected prior to the Battle of Gettysburg, having been built during the early 1840s. Today the home, which sits on Baltimore Street near Cemetery Hill, serves as a museum and plays host to hundreds of thousands of guests every year. By day you can learn all about its rich history, and the tragic events which occurred inside the walls on July 3, 1863; by night, however, you are invited to join the spirits that so many believe still roam freely through the house.

Mary Virginia Wade, erroneously nicknamed Jennie by a local newspaper, was the only civilian casualty during the battle. Jennie, then twenty years old, was staying in the home rented by her sister, Georgie Wade McClellan. Also in the home during the three-day battle were Mary Ann Felby Wade (Jennie's mother), Harry Wade (Jennie's brother), Louis McClellan (Georgia's newborn baby boy), and Isaac Brinkerhoff (a six-year-old boy not related to the family whom Jennie looked after to raise some extra money for the financially struggling family). Ironically when the two opposing forces collided in Gettysburg, Jennie made the decision to vacate the family home, located on Breckenridge Street, and fled to what she thought would be the safer of the two homes. Unfortunately, that decision would ultimately cost Jennie her life.

Upon arriving at her sister's home, the seemingly endless work began immediately. Repeated knocks at the door from Union soldiers asking for food and water prompted Jennie to do everything she could to help, including providing fresh water from the well. As the battle raged on through the first and second days of July, a continuous barrage of bullets banged against the outside of their home, and occasionally a bullet would fly in through a door or window. Jennie not only had to be worried for herself, but also for her family, as well as Isaac. As July 3rd dawned, the fighting continued to intensify in and around her once peaceful town.

Nearing exhaustion on the morning of the third, Jennie once again got started early, preparing breakfast for the rest of her family. Taking a break, she opened her Bible and did her customary daily reading, all the while continuing to hear the sounds of the violent and deadly battle exploding just outside their Baltimore Street abode. During her reading, an eerie foreshadowing of what was to come came out of her mouth, possibly some of the last words she ever spoke, "If there is anyone in this house that is to be killed today, I hope it is me, as Georgia has that little baby."

Around seven o'clock in the morning, the home once again seemed to be the center point of the gunfire. It did not take long for every pane of glass to be shattered by the bullets. One bullet entered the parlor room, struck the bedpost, hit the wall, and landed on a pillow on the bed in which Georgia and her baby boy were occupying. Scared for their lives, but realizing there was nothing they could do, they sat in fear, wondering what would happen next.

As the time neared eight thirty, Jennie stood in the kitchen, kneading dough for biscuits, when a single bullet fired by a Confederate soldier passed through two wooden doors, and struck the unsuspecting but fearful twenty-year-old just below her left shoulder blade. Sadly, the bullet pierced her heart, and killed her instantly. Mrs. Wade, a few steps away, turned and witnessed her beloved daughter fall to the floor dead. After seeing this, she calmly proceeded back into the parlor, and nonchalantly proclaimed, "Georgia, your sister is dead." In response to the unimaginable news, Georgia screamed so loudly and violently it prompted nearby Union soldiers to quickly enter the house and lead the surviving members of the family in a harrowing journey to save their own lives.

Was it possible Jennie Wade had a premonition of what was to come shortly before her death? Of course, the answer to that question will never be known. What is known, however, is that the parlor has provided some interesting and unexplainable happenings. One such incident occurred during my second year, and it involved a chamber pot sitting on the floor. What happened left investigators, and yours truly, awestruck.

While I loved sitting in on investigations, they can be long, tedious, and extremely frustrating. It is not unusual, in fact it is more the norm, to go minutes, hours, or days without experiencing an unexplained occurrence. What propels these enthusiasts to spend their time and hard-earned money on these often-underwhelming excursions? Do they do it for the money? Doubtful, as many investigation teams spend tens of thousands of dollars on just the equipment alone, not to mention the travel costs, food and lodging, missing time from their jobs, and the rental of the building they want to investigate.

The most frequent answer I got to this question, from the investigators themselves, was they simply did it for the excitement. The thrill of victory, no matter how unusual and infrequent it is, far outweighs the agony of defeat. The adrenaline rush that goes through your entire body the moment you realize you have captured something unexplainable is impossible to describe in words. Capturing something like that may only happen once in your life, if you are lucky, but the feeling you experience when you do is something you will never forget.

I was fortunate enough to be a part of hundreds of investigations during my five-year tenure. The investigative teams I was with ranged from two people to two dozen, or even more. I was with teams that did it for fun, and I was with teams that produced their own nationally syndicated television shows. Each group was unique, and no two investigations were ever the same. Many of the groups returned time after time, year after year, and I was fortunate enough to be requested by them each time they ventured back to Gettysburg.

One such group I met during my second year of doing tours was a group hailing from upstate New York, and they had their own arsenal of the most up-to-date ghost hunting equipment money could buy. Being with this particular team was a tremendous amount of fun. They were funny, friendly, and charismatic, and they were always emphatically serious about their investigations.

After doing my customary brief walkthrough presentation of the Jennie Wade House, it was time to get down to business. It took the team a little while to set up their equipment, but they reserved the building for the entire night, so time really was no concern for them. This was not their first investigation, so they certainly had their act together, and their game plan was well plotted out.

The group split up into several teams, going to different locations in the house; I remained with the team investigating the kitchen and parlor. The team I was with included the team captain, who tried for over an hour to elicit some sort of response from one or more of the spirits believed to be inhabiting the home.

His frustration grew as attempt after attempt proved futile. As the minutes continued to elapse, he eventually did something that was not unusual; he asked me to get involved. Even though it was only my second year doing tours and investigations, I had been in and out of the house hundreds of times and knew it like the back of my hand. Wasting no time, I began calling out, inviting whoever was with us to make their presence known.

Please keep in mind that even if the building is rented for the entire night, the paranormal groups renting the building only have a limited amount of time. They were not fortunate enough, like I was, to be able to return day after day, so because of this, they sought to maximize every moment they had while in the building. Yes, I was exhausted from a long week of working two jobs, but I had to remember these team members were there for a purpose, so I tried making it as enjoyable an experience as possible. I knew I had a job to do, the team had a job to do, and nothing or nobody was going to stop us. Or so we thought.

As I began my attempts to summons the spirits, there was a sense of frustration and doubt emanating from the team. I was saying the same things the team captain had just said for the past hour, so why would I be successful while he was not? Within seconds, however, something mind boggling happened.

"If there's anyone here with us right now, please do something to let us know," I casually announced, hoping for a response, but expecting nothing. "You know who I am. You know my voice, and you know I mean you no harm. It's just me and my friends here to talk to you."

Within seconds, the chamber pot, which was situated on the floor at the foot of the bed, slid approximately three feet. It is important for me to explain that the entire team and I were sitting on the floor, and nobody was even within arms-reach of the pot. In astonishment, we all sat speechless, waiting for some sort of explanation, but there was none.

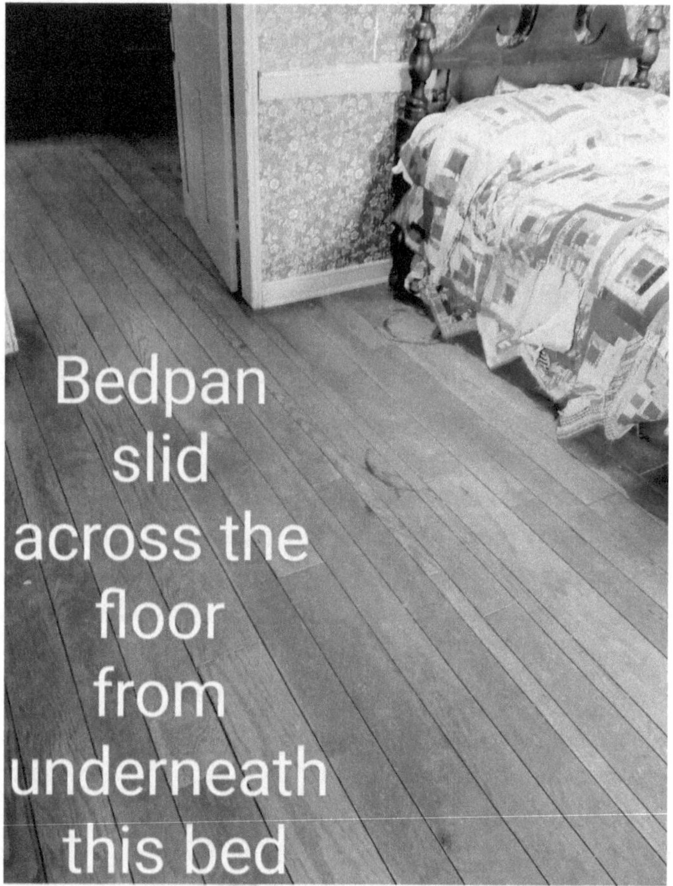

What happened in those early morning hours as five paranormal investigators and I sat on an old hardwood floor, trying to communicate with someone not of this world? Was this shocking turn of events simply a figment of all of our imaginations, stemming from the fact we were all tired beyond belief, or was someone or something trying to let us know that they were, in fact, there with us? All I can say is it *definitely* had our attention.

CHAPTER 4

I'M SORRY, I THOUGHT YOU WOULD WANT THE LIGHT ON

In March 2011, my second year, I began conducting tours through the orphanage. Admittedly, I was not overly familiar with the building and its tragic history prior to being a ghost tour guide. Wanting to be as well informed as possible before leading groups through the structure, I did a lot of research, including reading a book, One Soldier's legacy (Stouffer, Cindy A., and Collins, Mary Ruth. One Soldier's legacy; The National Homestead at Gettysburg. Gettysburg PA, Thomas Publications, 1996.) While my tours were not intended to be historical in nature, I always felt it was a plus to provide some background about the location my guests and I were walking through.

When the war initially began in 1861, many people believed it would only last for a few weeks, or a month or two at most. Instead, it carried on for four painstakingly long years, finally ending in April of 1865 when Lee surrendered at Appomattox Court House, Virginia. When all was said and done, approximately 620,000 soldiers lost their lives. As towns like Gettysburg struggled to properly deal with the mass of dead soldiers in their fields and streets, there was another significant problem: what would become of the children of the dead soldiers? With the fathers being killed, often the mothers were unable to financially support the family. With President Lincoln concentrating on reconstruction of the divided nation, the innocent children were often forgotten.

One year after the war ended, in 1866, the National Homestead at Gettysburg was opened. This gave some children a place to call home. Under the direction of Dr. Bourns of Philadelphia, Philinda Humiston, whose husband, Sergeant Amos Humiston of the 154th New York Regiment, was shot and killed on the first day of the battle, was named the first matron of the newly formed orphanage.

For the first three years the children, including Philinda and Amos' three children, flourished. They were healthy, well adjusted, and gradually healing from the trauma of losing a father and being separated from their mother. In 1869, as the number of children occupying the orphanage swelled, an adjacent building was added to accommodate the increasing numbers. The future was looking bright, and the children had a legitimate chance at a future, one which they very much deserved.

The children adored Philinda, and vice-versa. Unfortunately, in 1869, someone other than the children fell in love with the easy-going matron. Philinda ended up getting married and moving to Massachusetts with her new husband to start a new life, leaving the orphanage behind. Her departure would lead to disastrous consequences for the many children who considered the orphanage a second chance.

Dr. Bourns once again named a matron, a woman named Rosa J. Carmichael. With her at the helm, life at the orphanage changed dramatically, and not for the better. Rumors were rampant around town about the harsh conditions at the children's home, including how the orphans were being treated.

The precious children, who had already endured so much in their short lives, were kicked, beaten, and locked in their rooms or other areas in or around the orphanage. They were turned into personal slaves for Carmichael, being forced to do demeaning, subservient tasks. The children's self-esteem, which took Philinda three years to build up, was quickly torn down by the new head matron.

At times, the children were confined to "the Dungeon." The dungeon was a dark, windowless cell approximately five feet deep, eight feet wide, and four feet high. They were suspended by their arms in barrels and placed in shackles. Another cruel punishment Rosa would inflict was to force the teenage girls to wear boys' clothing. The psychological harm inflicted upon these already vulnerable children was equally as bad as the physical harm.

One such example of the torture was when a little girl was ordered to stand on top of a desk, in the same position, for so long she had to be lifted down when her punishment was over because she was suffering from pure exhaustion. Another trick of Rosa's was to blackmail the older teenage boys to be bullies to the younger, prepubescent children, disciplining them pursuant to Rosa's cruel instructions, and often violent demands.

Occasionally, the residents of Gettysburg would catch wind of the brutal conditions at the Baltimore Street orphanage, and would demand action. Investigators would show up at the property, but the children that were abused would be hidden out of sight until the investigations were completed. Rosa tricked so many for so long, but her luck would soon run out.

On a bitterly cold, windy day in December, on or about Christmas Eve, while most children around the world were nestled in their beds dreaming about the imminent arrival of Santa Claus, one young boy under Rosa's "care" was locked into an outhouse. Sadly, it was not just for a few minutes; he was subjected to the freezing cold Pennsylvania winter temperatures for quite some time. Becoming hysterical because of the conditions, he eventually let out blood-curdling screams for help. Thankfully his pleas were heard, and he was mercifully rescued by a concerned neighbor.

By the late 1870s, the number of children calling the orphanage their home dwindled to next to nothing, and the few that did remain were quickly adopted by the residents in and around Gettysburg. The Homestead ultimately ceased operations in 1877, putting an end to the atrocities perpetrated by Rosa Carmichael. The fact that she vehemently denied all charges against her was not surprising, given the evil person she was.

What happened to Rosa after the closure of the orphanage remains a mystery to this day. Where she went and when she died is unknown. Many believe she was in cahoots with Dr. Bourns, and quite possibly disappeared to somewhere in the Philadelphia area, where he was a prominent figure. Regardless, Mr. Bourns' knowledge, or lack thereof, of what happened to these poor children at the Homestead Orphanage continues to be debated.

Since its closing, the structure has witnessed numerous owners, the most famous of which happened to be by a man by the name of Charley Weaver, whose real name was Cliff Arquette, a famous comedian and actor known for his role in the popular television show, the Jack Parr show. Mr. Arquette purchased the property in 1957, and subsequently turned it into the Charley Weaver Museum of the Civil War, which opened in 1959. It later became known as The Soldiers National Museum.

Our tour company was blessed to have exclusive rights to conduct ghost tours in the building, and the experiences I personally encountered, or that happened during my tours, were countless. Throughout the remainder of this book, I will highlight some of my favorites, or most terrifying, depending on how you want to look at it.

Of all of them, one encounter startled me the most, and made me rethink my entire approach while inside the orphanage. The incident occurred in the cellar of the building, prior to any tours being conducted on that day. It was a Saturday, one in which I will never forget.

Anyone who has taken any of my tours knows how loud and animated I get. I am proud to conclude that not a single guest of mine had any trouble hearing what I was saying. Was I too loud at times? Quite possibly, but for the most part, people loved my enthusiasm and drive, as evidenced by the many positive Trip Advisor reviews I got throughout my five years.

During my ventures into the orphanage, either for tours or investigations, I never backed away from calling out Rosa. I did not hesitate in letting her know my total disdain toward her. A sampling of the words I often used to describe her included cruel, sinister, evil, and I even went so far as to calling her a heartless bitch. It was not unusual for me to ask her why she did the deplorable things she did to the precious children, who had already been through hell in their short lives. I also challenged her to try and bully me like she did them, and I chastised her for not having the fortitude (guts) to pick on someone her own size. I have no doubt whatsoever my constant belittling of her struck a nerve.

Just like the other tours in town, our tours normally did not start until the evening. The belief amongst our guests was ghosts only come out at night, and this common belief suited me just fine as I truly believe this historic town of Gettysburg, especially during the day, should be all about the history and the soldiers who sacrificed their lives in order to ensure all men are created equal. Our nighttime ghost tours simply gave the visitors of Gettysburg something to do at night when the battlefield was off limits.

On weekends I would normally arrive at our shop early. I loved talking to guests, and they, in turn, loved sharing their paranormal experiences with me. A friendly word or two often brightened the day of the tourists in Gettysburg walking up and down the sidewalks, and frequently led to them wanting to take a ghost tour with our company. I made hundreds of friends simply by extending my hand for a handshake, and exchanging a genuine smile.

One particular Saturday I arrived early, and was asked by my boss to go down into the cellar of the orphanage to change a light bulb that had blown out in the hallway leading back into the dungeon. Since we permitted our guests to go back into that area, and even crawl into the pit during the tour, it was important that the hallway was properly lit in order to avoid injury. Happy to help out while waiting for my tours to begin, I walked down the old, creaky wooden steps into the cellar. After opening the door to the hallway, I turned the lights on, and immediately noticed the first light was out.

As I was unscrewing the light bulb, I noticed through my peripheral vision that the door that I had opened about thirty seconds earlier was quickly closing. As it slammed shut with a loud thud, my initial thought was that either my boss, or another tour guide, was playing a trick on me, which was not unusual. However, after assessing the situation, I quick realized that was not the case. Anyone who has ascended or descended the steps leading to and from the cellar knows that, due to the condition of the steps (age, wear), every step taken is unmistakably audible, so I knew I would have definitely heard someone coming down the steps. Realizing that, I started to panic.

Making matters worse was the fact that this incident occurred shortly after a group of guests and their tour guide were inexplicably locked in the cellar and had to patiently wait for the tour guide to use her cellphone to summon another tour guide to come and let them out. That was a harrowing incident for all involved.

After my initial thought of simply being the victim of a practical joke, Rosa getting revenge on me started filling my brain. I could not stop thinking about how, just a century-and-a-half earlier, she locked those innocent children in that same area I was now occupying. Had she had enough of me bad talking her every chance I got?

Trying to keep my composure, I made the determination that if, in fact, I was ultimately locked in, my two-hundred-pound body would be breaking right through that old, wooden door. Thankfully, for both my sake and the door's, the door was not locked, and I proceeded to break the land-speed record getting the hell out of that hallway, up the steps, and far away from the cellar. Already knowing the answer, but just to cover all my bases, I asked my boss if he or one of the other tour guides had come down and slammed the door shut on me. He simply responded, "No."

Why and how did the door slam shut on its own? Was Rosa trying to make a statement or giving me a stern warning to back off? Perhaps my thinking was incorrect, and one of the spirits of the orphaned children slammed it shut, having some fun at my expense. Whatever the answer, which will never be known, every subsequent time I walked down into that cellar, especially when I was alone, I would think about that Saturday afternoon. I can proudly say, however, I never did back off my verbal attack of one Rosa J. Carmichael. As harrowing as the experience was, it was a mere foreshadowing of what was to come.

CHAPTER 5

PLAYTIME OR RETALIATION?

Unlike today, identifying the fallen soldiers during the Civil War was extremely difficult. When the three-day battle had concluded on July 3, 1863, the two sides wasted no time in getting out of Gettysburg. Sadly, the brave soldiers who lost their lives were left behind, and with every passing day, week, and even month, the dead soldiers' true identities remained a mystery. The only distinguishable identifier was the color of the uniform the soldiers wore, which signified what side that particular soldier fought for.

One such example of an unidentified soldier was the story of Sergeant Amos Humiston, who was killed on July 1, 1863. What made the Humiston account so unique and tragic was the fact that when his body was found, he was clutching a blood-stained photograph of three young children, two boys and a girl.

The citizens of Gettysburg were moved by the discovery of this soldier and the children contained in the photograph. The locals knew that this hero's thoughts as he took his last breath, were, most likely, of the children. Were they his children? Nobody knew. In fact, nobody knew who this soldier even was. The only thing that was known about this soldier was he fought for the Union. Heartbroken, the residents of Gettysburg wanted to identify this proud northerner, and return the photo to the family of the children who just lost their father. Without dog tags (listing the soldier's name, social security number, and blood type, amongst other things), which are utilized today for identification purposes, finding the rightful home of the photograph was going to be difficult, if not impossible.

Doctor John F. Bourns, a volunteer battlefield surgeon, stepped in, took possession of the picture, and made thousands of copies to distribute to various media publications. His goal was for someone who knew this soldier's identity to step forward. While it did not happen overnight, eventually his goal became a reality when, approximately four months later, Philinda Humiston of Portville, New York, came forward and identified the children in the photograph as being her children, Frank, Alice, and Frederick. She had previously sent the photograph to her husband, Sergeant Amos Humiston. While heartbroken on learning of her husband's demise, it is certain she was finally able to get some closure, and took solace in the fact that he had his children on his mind, close to his heart, when he passed away.

Mrs. Humiston later moved herself and the three children to Gettysburg, and fittingly became the first matron of the National Homestead at Gettysburg. Assisting her in this endeavor was the aforementioned Dr. Bourns, who was the founder and supervisor. Ironically, Philinda and her three children lived adjacent to the cemetery in which her husband was buried.

During Philinda's tenure as matron, the children at the Homestead were happy, and well taken care of. They played an active and integral role in the community, participating in patriotic holidays. One of the highlights of the children's participation was the Memorial Day holiday, when the orphans would place flags on the soldier's gravesites. It was quite possible that some of the children placed flags on their own father's gravesite. Since the children were so well-behaved and polite, the local residents enjoyed seeing and interacting with them. But as usual, all good things had to come to an end, and a screeching halt they did.

As previously mentioned, Philinda left the Homestead, and Rosa Carmichael took the reins, and when that happened, the exuberance of the children disappeared. Rosa Carmichael was the true definition of evil "see chapter 4". They went from being a visible staple of the community, to being isolated, and confined to the Homestead. The proverbial tip of the iceberg came in May of 1876 during the Memorial Day holiday. Normally a major part of the festivities, the youngsters were noticeably absent, which infuriated the townspeople. It was after this intentional snub by Rosa that questions began to be raised about what exactly was going on in the orphanage, which just so happened to be the temporary headquarters of Union Major General Oliver Howard during the battle itself.

Is it not ironic how totally different two people can be? Amos Humiston fought and died for his country; his final thoughts being of his beloved children, while on the opposite end of the spectrum was Rosa Carmichael, an evil, demented abuser (both physically and psychologically) of her position of authority in the most heinous ways possible.

Of particular interest to me is a toy table which sits in the cellar of the orphanage. Guests on my ghost tours were familiar with the story behind the toys on the table, and this story touched them so much, it was not unusual for them to bring toys back on their return trips to Gettysburg and place them on the table. The guests, and I myself, believe the orphans still play in that cellar to this day, and are hopeful that these toys bring some joy to them.

Toys left on the table ranged anywhere from Matchbox cars to stuffed animals, picture books, coloring books, crayons, and even a candy bar or two. Our kind-hearted guests always told me they wanted to bring some joy and happiness back to the children, much like the children had during the Philinda Humiston days.

It was not uncommon for a bouncy ball to mysteriously fall off the table, or toys to be moved around, especially when I would turn out the lights just prior to the tour ending. Sitting or standing in the cellar, and even in the pit, while the lights were extinguished, was always a super popular aspect of my tours, one which was always heavily anticipated by the guests. One such incident, however, sticks out more so than the others.

Many guests enjoy visiting Gettysburg in mid spring, from late April to early May. While at times there may still be a chill in the air, the long, arduous, bitterly cold months of winter are in the rear-view mirror, and with each passing day, the sun sparkles high in the sky a little longer. Schools have yet to close for summer vacation, which means the crowds are smaller more manageable, and more tolerable for those who enjoy a serene atmosphere. Instead of the usual twenty to twenty-five guests that make the journey into the orphanage during the busy months, only about half that number make their way inside during this time of year.

On a Thursday evening in mid-May, which was just prior to the start of the busy season, an incident occurred that no one in the tour group, nor myself, would soon forget. It took the lure of the toy table to a whole new level, and not a single plausible explanation could be made of what happened. That evening, similar to any other orphanage tour I did, I gave anyone on the tour group the opportunity to venture back down the hallway to the dungeon. After opening the door that separated the main portion of the cellar and the hallway, the group, which consisted of adults only, made their way back. Everyone walked back ahead of me, but only approximately half of the group wriggled their way into the pit itself.

We spent about ten minutes in the hallway and pit area before I escorted the group back out into the main portion of the cellar. Leading the group, I stepped out of the hallway, down the step, and immediately tripped over something on the floor, causing me to fall. Believing that my ankle was sprained and I was seriously hurt, several guests came rushing to my aid, helping me up off the floor. When I looked to see what I had stepped on, I noticed a green spinning top sitting in the middle of the floor, in front of the step.

When everyone was once again seated, and had settled down, we talked about the toys. Being one of larger toys on the table, I noticed the top many times. We all agreed the toy was definitely not sitting on the floor in front of the step prior to us walking back the hallway. In fact, one of the guests showed me a picture she had taken of the toy table before we stepped foot in the hallway, and the top was sitting on the table.

As mentioned in chapter 4, if someone would have come down the steps, one of the guests, or myself, would have heard the sound of steps creaking. Furthermore, all of the guests went with me back down the hallway that night, which was unusual as normally a few guests remain in the main portion of the cellar. I was the last person walking down the hallway, but was the first person coming back out. At some point during the time that we had walked down the hallway, the top went from the table to the floor.

We were all shocked by this turn of events. Since we were the only group in the orphanage that evening, I invited the guests to stick around and talk about what had happened. Every guest remained, and they all wanted an explanation from me, which I struggled to provide. Confused myself, I offered two possible explanations: first, one of the orphan's wanted to play with the top and thought it would be easier to spin it while it was sitting on the floor. If this was the case, I believe there was no malice behind it. The second scenario, however, is that Rosa Carmichael purposely moved the toy from the table, strategically placing it where she knew I would step down. Some of the guests did not believe the evil matron was that intuitive to manufacture a sinister deed like that, but those guests were quickly reminded how Rosa perpetrated the atrocities against the children for years before anybody found out about it. No matter what, or who, was behind moving the top, I learned a valuable lesson that night: always look before stepping down from the hallway in that cellar.

Sometimes spirits can be wicked and depraved, like Rosa Carmichael. But some spirits, like the fabled Johnny Reb, are confused, overwhelmed, mischievous, and most of all, stuck in time.

CHAPTER 6

LADIES AND GENTLEMEN: JOHNNY REB

It was the start of my third year of conducting tours, and I was doing just about every tour our company had to offer. The exception, however, was the newly created ghostly encounter tours, which were extremely popular. What exactly is a ghostly encounter tour? In simple terms, it is a tour in which your tour guide is a ghost.

When the ghostly encounter tours were introduced, they consisted only of the orphanage tour, wherein the tour guide portrayed the infamous Rosa Carmichael. The two guides who conducted this tour were phenomenal, and they truly deserved the accolades they had received for their portrayal of this evil person.

The Rosa Carmichael Orphanage Ghostly Encounter Tour routinely sold out, and our guests wanted more. The concept was original and added to our prestige of being one of the most popular tour companies in Gettysburg. Our manager was a creative genius, always thinking up new tours to offer to the public, and with this new specialty tour, he had hit a home run.

Meanwhile, I was plugging along, doing my various tours, and loving every minute of it. By my third year, I had a tremendous number of followers, and was often requested by our repeat guests, which I took as a great testimony, but I wanted more. Doing the introductions for other tour guides, I witnessed firsthand the popularity of our newest tour, and I wanted to be a part of it.

I was fully aware that doing that type of tour in the orphanage, being a grown man in his early forties, was nearly impossible. Who could I have been? Dr. Bourns? Rosa's husband (who knows if any man ever even wanted her?) One of the boys who stayed at the orphanage? Realizing the opportunities were far more limited in the orphanage, I quickly shifted gears, and began weighing the possibilities of utilizing the Jennie Wade House as a backdrop.

When I approached my manager with this idea, he was more than receptive, which made me ecstatic. Agreeing that it was a good idea, he instructed me to write a script for his review. While I had hoped he would like the idea, I never dreamed he would ask me to write it myself. Because I had a tremendous amount of respect for our manager, I was honored, and immediately began brainstorming.

Between my full-time job and doing more tours than I had ever done, my time was limited. To say I was stretched out would be an understatement, but I was so excited, I set aside time every day to work on it. My degree in creative writing was finally starting to pay dividends, and I could not have been happier. I was going to produce, and star in, my own ghostly encounter tour!

It took me several months to complete the script. I knew I had to create a character that would grab people's attention, just like Rosa did in the ghostly encounter orphanage tour. There were so many ghost tours in town already, so if I wanted my creation to be successful, it had to be unique, emphatic, and even splashy.

After considerable deliberation, and knowing Jennie Wade's death was really the only option I had, I came up with the story of the unknown Confederate soldier who fired the fateful bullet on July 3, 1863, piercing Jennie's heart, killing her instantly. My initial concern, however, had to do with whether I could turn this subject into a ninety-minute tour. I soon came up with an answer.

No one has ever identified the soldier who fired the shot; therefore, I created a fictional character that, after long consideration and reflection, named Johnny Reb. Crazy Johnny Reb was a soldier who lost his life during Pickett's Charge, and since then found himself stuck in time. He had been (and was still being) accused, whether fairly or unfairly, of firing the bullet that killed Jennie Wade. His one and only mission was to clear his name and prove her blood was not on his hands.

My main goal in creating the character was to have as many different, and complex, attitudes and emotions that I could possibly come up with, and I wholeheartedly believe I succeeded. Johnny was angry because he was stuck in present day Gettysburg, and to compound matters, he was constantly being blamed for Jennie's death.

Johnny Reb was tastefully insulting. I had to be careful not to go too over the top, or I would turn people off, so I would slip in an occasional "duh" to a guest, or sporadically hurl a name at them such as "simpleton" (my favorite) or "dunderhead." I knew with these minor and nonpersonal insults, I was not turning people against me as a tour guide.

Another aspect of Johnny I wanted to exhibit was his sorrowfulness. While he defended himself to the end, he could not argue that an innocent young lady had been shot and killed. A perfect example of his emotional instability was when he was standing in the kitchen, exactly where she was shot and killed, and he would drop down on his knees to the floor, slap his hands down (which I did it with such force it actually hurt on several occasions), wailing out, "Why were you standing here!? Why! Why!" This was an exceptionally dramatic portion of the tour, often leaving the guests speechless.

I also wanted him to have a bit of a sense of humor. I wanted him to be a comedian, at least in his own mind. It was not unusual for him to blurt out, "I crack myself up." Another one of his famous lines had to do with the group crossing Baltimore Street when there were no more "horseless carriages" coming in either direction.

Mischievousness also had to be a driving trait of his. The devilish pranks he would often perform included goggling at the guests, picking on people who were not part of the tour, and puffing his chest out at guests, especially when they would turn their backs on him. He tended to pick out a guest and torment him or her (always tastefully) throughout the entire tour.

In my creation of Johnny Reb, I wanted him to go to the opposite ends of the emotional spectrum. The exact opposite of humor and mischievousness was confusion, and if Johnny Reb had a middle name, that would have been it. He was often in a state of total bewilderment, continuously asking the guests why they blamed him for "Miss Ginny's death?" On a lighter note, he could never figure out today's "fandangle contraptions," such as "the thing you, and everyone else, is holding in your hands, and constantly pushing buttons, or holding it up to your ear while also talking into it at the same time."

He grieved the loss of his brother who died right in front of his eyes on the second day of the Battle of Gettysburg while charging up East Cemetery Hill. "The last thing Momma said to me as we left the house was 'you take care of your little brother for your Momma, Johnny. You keep him safe no matter what.' I'm sorry Momma, I was standing right there beside him when a damn minnie ball nearly took his head right off his shoulders. There was nothing I could do!" he would cry out, while once again falling to his knees, silencing the guests.

Desperation was yet another of his driving characteristics. Throughout the ninety-minute tour, he would try to convince even the most headstrong disbelievers of his innocence. That he was, in fact, not guilty as charged. The most common phrase he would utter, repeatedly, was, "I didn't do it. You believe me, don't you?"

Johnny was hungry for sympathy. He wanted the guests to know that he lost his own life mere hours after Jennie did, marching across the open fields on General George Pickett's orders. "Everybody cares so much about her, but what about me?" he questioned while having a sad, depressed, devastated look on his face.

Finally, he was loyal, as so many of his fellow soldiers were. He loved the Confederate States of America and fought with all he could give until taking his final breath. He loved whistling "Dixie" while walking from one spot to the next, and tried to encourage guests to do the same. What was most apparent, however, was his love, admiration, and dedication to his beloved leader, General Robert E. Lee. He was profoundly proud that he got to see his hero riding past him on Traveler (his horse) just hours before he was killed. "The confidence General Lee had in me, in all of us, made us want to fight even harder for him," he would say as his voice cracked.

One of my personal favorite songs of all times is "Bohemian Rhapsody" by Queen. Listening to the five minute, forty-one second tune, I've always been amazed at the conflicting styles within the classic itself. It starts out slow and quiet, almost soothing. The middle transitions into an up tempo, anything-but-relaxing, on-the-edge-of-your-seat melody, at one point reaching a high note many could not imagine attaining. Near the end of the song, it reverts back to the tranquility from the song's beginning. That whole concept was what I was aiming for with Johnny Reb. I wanted the ups and downs, the conflicting emotions, to be at the opposite ends of the spectrum, and I sincerely believe he manifested that every time he put on the uniform and ventured out into the courtyard to begin his adventure.

———◆———

Having completed the manuscript, I submitted it to my manager for his review and approval. With only a few minor changes, it was time to rehearse. Yes, I had a product on paper, but before presenting it to the public, there was still a considerable amount of work to be done. I had a twelve-page script to carry out in a ninety-minute time period.

Practice makes perfect, and while I was (and still am) far from that, I spent countless hours trying to perfect my creation. Luckily for me I had unlimited access to the Jennie Wade House, so I was able to actually go inside the home to rehearse. Every day for three straight weeks I did dry runs by myself. During the week I would drive from my full-time job to Gettysburg just to do a run through, or two. If I had a tour that night, I would stay in Gettysburg after my rehearsal, and if not, I drove home. On the weekends I would go early prior to my tours. I cannot imagine how I must have looked standing alone in the field behind the Jennie Wade House talking to myself. I am surprised nobody ever had me committed.

When I felt ready, it was time to perform. Because I wanted to appear as authentic as possible, I dressed up in full Confederate uniform, including wool pants and jacket, white shirt, suspenders, kepi, and even brogans. The brogans I had were extremely slippery, so I had to be extra careful not to slip and fall. I wore the same uniform no matter how hot the temperature. It was not unusual on a sizzling hot summer night for me to sweat off several pounds. I also carried a replica rifle, which I obtained permission from the local police department to carry.

Setting the tone quickly in the courtyard, I would accuse the guests of seeking me out, blaming me for a crime I did not commit. My demeanor was filled with anger, and by judging my guests' reactions early, I could determine who I could playfully banter back and forth with, which would last throughout the entire tour. I remember one instance, however, in which my judgment was wrong. A female guest came to me early on in the tour and informed me she did not appreciate being called a simpleton. I appreciated her coming to me, one on one, while the other guests were occupied, so I apologized, and picked a different guest to squabble with. I wanted my guests to have a good time, an unforgettable experience, so hurting someone's feelings, or offending anyone, was certainly not my objective.

Following a no-nonsense introduction, Johnny would lead the group out of the old village, across Baltimore Street, and into the grassy area behind the Jennie Wade House. Telling the guests he was a member of the most feared battalion of the confederacy, the Louisiana Tigers, Johnny would describe how, on the second evening of the battle, his "Fighting Tigers" stormed up the hill, passing right through where the group was standing at that particular moment, and attacked the "Yankees" on East Cemetery Hill. It was a rare after-dark attack carried out by the Confederates in an effort to try and seize control of the important high ground, but after a "valiant effort, we were turned back, forced to retreat right back through here, while dodging the bullets that whistled past our heads, all the while trying not to trip over all of the dead bodies lying on the ground, especially where you're standing."

Since the Johnny Reb tour was a ghost tour, before leaving the field I would tell the story about a girl who was on vacation with her parents. While the family was staying at the motel adjacent to the Jennie Wade House, she constantly witnessed soldiers, who she assumed were reenactors, wandering around the grassy area in which the group was currently standing. When the girl would excitedly summon her parents to come look, the soldiers seemed to disappear. The father thought his daughter was fabricating the whole story, possibly seeking attention, so he took her by the hand and led her to the field. Once they arrived at their destination, the father and daughter duo experienced a terrifying ordeal. While I will not go into detail and tell the story here (it's not mine to tell), I will tell you Johnny loved this portion of the tour because he was able to get one of the youngsters involved, which was a favorite of theirs.

Following his stop in the field, Johnny would lead the group back through the parking lot and around to the north side of the house, stopping at the door which contained the bullet hole. After his version of what happened on the morning of July 3rd, he escorted the group into the kitchen. Because the kitchen was where Jennie was shot and killed, Johnny had trouble containing his emotions.

Leaving the kitchen, the group proceeded into the parlor, then up the wooden steps to the second floor of the home where they walked through the knocked-down wall separating the two sides of the home. They continued into the McClain side, went down the steps, into the parlor and kitchen, and finally ended up in the cellar where Jennie's dead body remained until after the battle ended. This progression was the exact route the family took on July 3, 1863, in order to avoid danger themselves.

Throughout the home, Johnny would give his version of what happened. While the information and history he supplied was accurate, he had the tendency to manipulate some of the facts in order to support his "side of the story."

Once in the cellar, the guests were finally able to sit down after being on their feet for over an hour. Johnny would always get into a one-sided argument with James Wade, Jennie's father, as to whether or not he was the one who pulled the trigger, killing Jennie. Johnny would emphasize to him that James wife Mary, Jennie's mother, had him declared "very insane" and committed into the Alms House in Gettysburg, where he lived during the battle and his daughter's death. Johnny would also point out how James spent two years in solitary confinement at the Eastern State Penitentiary in Philadelphia, Pennsylvania, for larceny.

Johnny did not hesitate in calling Mr. Wade out, challenging him to a dual. When that happened, he would turn the lights out, allowing the guests to sit in the scariest portion of the home in complete darkness, which was a favorite of many guests. The younger children, of course, were not a huge fan of the lights being turned out and would often snuggle up to their parents, scared out of their minds.

When the lights came back on, Johnny Reb was gone, and I was the tour guide. I would take the few remaining minutes of the tour to explain that Johnny Reb was, in fact, a fictional character that yours truly had created. I further explained that while it was a Confederate soldier who fired the bullet, nobody, including the shooter himself, knew what had happened. The sad truth of it was that the only civilian killed during the Battle of Gettysburg was not a target, but was in the wrong place, at the wrong time.

I thought it was equally important to chronicle Jennie's pilgrimage after her tragic death; her body being moved from the cellar to the garden behind the house (which is now the gift shop), where it remained for approximately six months. In January 1864, her body was once again moved, this time to a cemetery next to a German Reform Church in Gettysburg, and subsequently moved in 1865 to its final resting spot in the Evergreen Cemetery, where her grave is marked by a monument and an American flag.

At the conclusion of every tour, whether it was the regular walking tours or the Johnny Reb tours, I stuck around for a question and answer session, and for photos. Guests loved having their pictures taken with crazy Johnny Reb, who allowed them to wear his hat and hold his rifle. It was not unusual for Johnny to strike an uncanny pose for the camera.

Not only was Johnny a part of the Ghostly Encounter tours, but he also partook in the popular Midnight in A Haunted House spectacular offered every Saturday night during the season. From time to time, he would also appear at a campground, another tour, and even a fundraising event.

Out of all the tours I conducted, portraying Johnny Reb was, by far, my favorite. The overall theme of the tour remained the same, but every tour was different. I played off the guests; the more they reacted, the more I did. I never got bored with Johnny Reb. I loved acting, storytelling, and people, so this was the perfect combination, and the success of this tour proved it.

Speaking of people, during my two-and-a-half years of doing the Ghostly Encounter tour, I met some of the most amazing, kindest guests one could ever imagine. I formed lasting friendships, and even a relationship or two. These people were as loyal as they come, and I will never forget them. I count my blessings every day for them, and with them created memories that will last forever, some of which I mention in the next chapter.

CHAPTER 7

FRIENDS MAKE THE WORLD GO AROUND

Without a shadow of a doubt, my favorite part of doing the tours was the opportunity to meet new people. The tens of thousands of guests I met throughout my five years, and the smiles I put on (most of) their faces, made it all worthwhile. Our company's loyal visitors worked hard all year long to be able to relax and enjoy their vacation, and I was honored so many guests wanted to include me as part of their plans.

In doing the tours, I met people from all walks of life. These people came from every corner of the United States, and beyond. The close-knit bonds I formed with many of them will never be broken, and I have only them to thank. I will forever be indebted for the kindness and loyalty they exhibited, and I look forward to our continued friendships.

How were so many friendships formed? My answer is that I absolutely loved what I did, and the guests knew it. It did not matter to me if there was only one guest on the tour, or twenty-five, I always put forth my best effort. Our paying guest(s) deserved that. It made no difference to me if we were sitting around a campfire or in the middle of a Johnny Reb Tour, my enthusiasm did not wane.

One thing I began doing early my first year was, after my tour ended, inviting the guests to stick around and showing them pictures previous guests sent me that were taken during one of my tours. The percentage of guests who stuck around was always mind boggling to me. These people just listened to me talk for ninety minutes or longer, but they wanted more, and I was honored. It was not unusual for us to stand outside the Jennie

Wade House Gift Shop for an hour or more, talking, laughing, and having a good time. We would reminisce about what happened on the tour, and they always wanted to hear about my most interesting encounters. It was during these after-tour moments that many of the friendships were formed.

Whether a guest stuck around or not, I always provided a business card to each of them who wanted one with some of my personal information. I did this in case anyone wanted to keep in touch with me. In this day and age, nearly everyone has email, Facebook, Twitter, Instagram, Snapchat, or some other form of social media, and I had all of them. I was always pleasantly surprised the number of guests that did, in fact, keep in contact.

In this chapter, I will provide an incomplete list of amazing people I was fortunate enough to meet and become friends with during my ghost tours. I say it is an incomplete list because it would be impossible for me to go through and list all of them (I would fill up sets of encyclopedias if I did that). If you are reading this book, please do not get offended if I failed to mention your name. In reality, you are equally important to me, and I truly treasured each and every one of you.

My first year as a tour guide, I focused primarily on the Jennie Wade House. During one of my midweek tours, I met a father (Eric), son (Joel), and daughter (Kennedy), from upstate New York. The three had been coming to Gettysburg their entire lives, and thoroughly enjoyed taking ghost tours. They went on my Jennie Wade tour and enjoyed it so much they stuck around afterward to talk. Kennedy seemed very intrigued with the ghost tour and was full of questions regarding my personal experiences. As I said goodbye to the family that evening, I was not sure if and when I would see them again. My uncertainty, however, was quickly answered.

The following morning, they called our gift shop, and asked if I was doing a tour that night. Receiving the answer they were hoping for, they reserved three tickets for that evening's tour. Despite doing the exact same tour the previous evening, they were once again guests of my Jennie Wade Tour. Similar to the previous night, they stuck around after the tour, and this time Kennedy had an extensive list of questions ready for me. Two hours later, we parted ways once again.

Following their return to New York, we remained in contact with each other, becoming good friends. They would come to Gettysburg three or four times every year, and would take multiple tours with me. They did not care what tour I was offering that particular evening; they were quick to make reservations.

Each time they were in Gettysburg, we would get together outside of the ghost tour setting. We would often have lunch or dinner, and Kennedy would always have questions ready for me. Our favorite place to meet while they were in town was Friendly's, and of course we would always make a trip or two out to the Sachs Covered Bridge, which is also known as one of the most haunted locations in Gettysburg "see Chapter 8 for the story of this famous haunted bridge".

They would usually reserve one of our buildings for an investigation and would ask me to investigate with them. The hours the four of us spent in the Jennie Wade House are countless, and we had incredible times together. I looked forward to their trips to Gettysburg year after year, and I loved seeing Joel and Kennedy grow up. Joel was a high school student when we first met and he ended up attending Gettysburg College after his high school graduation, while Kennedy went from a shy tween to a bold, fearless, beautiful young lady.

During one of their trips to Gettysburg, they introduced me to something I had never done before, in fact I had never even heard of: geocaching. Traveling around with them through the historical town's countryside searching for hidden trinkets or other objects was a blast, and something I ended up doing with my own daughter and her friends.

They also took me to places in Gettysburg that, incredibly, I never knew existed, and vice-versa. After the tours, we would often visit the Cashtown Inn, Sachs Covered Bridge, Little Round Top, and many, many more places in and around the town. I always looked forward to their visits, and I knew our adventures would be limitless.

I loved hearing how Joel would play Dixie on his phone every time they entered Gettysburg. It was a tradition second-to-none. As soon as he did that, he would text me announcing their arrival. Eric would always bring me a generous supply of Loganberry, a popular non-carbonated drink found primarily in the northern New York area. I love the drink and continue to be disappointed it cannot be found in the south-central Pennsylvania area. Unfortunately, the tasty drink never lasted long in my refrigerator.

Our get togethers were not just limited to Gettysburg. Every winter during Christmas break I would take a day and go visit them. I would check the weather forecast before leaving (upstate New York gets a LOT of snow), but it was a trip I looked forward to every year. Whenever I visited them, they made sure I got to see some of their countryside. We would normally grab something to eat at (you guessed it) Friendly's before I would leave to return home. We always had a great time together.

When Kennedy landed a lead role in her school's musical, she invited me to attend, and I could not disappoint. At the time I was coaching my daughter's basketball team, and as luck would have it, we had a morning game that day. Taking my obligation to her third-grade basketball team seriously, and knowing I could not miss Kennedy's musical, I decided to do both.

Immediately after the basketball game ended, a game in which we won, I jumped in my car and drove the six plus hours, nonstop, to see her perform. With just a few minutes to spare, I settled into her school's auditorium and was pleasantly surprised with her Oscar-like performance. My initial plan was to spend the night at their house, but there was a winter storm moving into the area, so after a hearty dinner at McDonalds, I headed home. I spent nearly thirteen hours on the road for a two-hour musical, but I would most definitely do it all over again.

Unfortunately, due to circumstances, and no fault of Eric's, we have lost contact with each other. While we may no longer communicate, I will never forget the times his family and I spent together, and I sincerely hope we are able to reconnect at some point in the near future.

⎯⎯•⎯⎯

A youngster by the name of Tony F., from Lancaster County, Pennsylvania (located about sixty to seventy-five minutes from Gettysburg) was diagnosed at six days old with a very rare digestive disorder. Years later, Tony needed transplant surgery to save his life, but he had to wait for the perfect match. Tony was dealt this unimaginable blow, but never allowed it to affect who he was.

One Saturday night during my first year of doing tours, Tony and his amazing family took my Jennie Wade Tour. I immediately recognized how this young man had the most incredible attitude. Most adults would not handle adversity the way he did, and I did everything I could to make sure he and his family's trips to Gettysburg were made as memorable as possible. He was a true inspiration to me, and I made sure he knew it.

Similar to Eric and his family, Tony and his family came to Gettysburg several times every year. Young Tony, along with his brothers and parents, always had a smile on their faces, which impressed me to the core. They would not allow Tony's condition to get in their way. Whenever they traveled to Gettysburg, they always took in one of my tours. While I treated every tour, and every guest, as unique, I always had an extra bounce in my step when Tony was on my tour.

His parents, two of the kindest people I have ever met, threw an annual fundraiser to raise money for medical expenses for their son. The event would happen in October and take place at the Lancaster Barnstormer's minor league baseball stadium. I was privileged, and blessed, to be invited to this event every year. I entertained the audience with ghost stories, trying to help raise money on his behalf. It was truly uplifting for me to see the overwhelming support for this young man, and I always wished I could do more. There is not a day that goes by I don't think about Tony and his family. I understand he eventually received the transplant he so desperately needed and deserved, and my advice to Tony is keep smiling, my friend.

⬥

Shannon C. was also from Pennsylvania, and she too enjoyed visiting Gettysburg several times a year. Whenever she did venture to Gettysburg, she always made it a point to take at least one of my tours. While she enjoyed the Jennie Wade Tour, and my Johnny Reb Tour, her favorite was the orphanage tour. Even when she wasn't in Gettysburg, Shannon and I stayed in contact with each other via Facebook and texting. What I remember most about her was she was smart, funny, driven, and had a radiant smile.

⬥

Since Ohio borders Pennsylvania, we got quite a few guests from the Buckeye State. Charles S. and his son and daughter were three of those guests. The first time I met the trio was when they took my orphanage tour. Midway through the tour, Charles approached me and explained they were leaving. They were not dissatisfied with the tour, and in fact he was loving it, but his son was frightened. He apologized, which there was absolutely no reason to, and as they were leaving the building, he made sure to tell me they would be back someday, and would try taking my tour again.

One year later, they returned to Gettysburg and insisted on taking one of my tours. As luck would have it, I was doing the same orphanage tour they had departed in the middle of the year before. Both Charles and I were concerned, but in this case, one year made all the difference. Not only did both of his children make it through the entire tour, they loved it. Charles was more than thrilled he finally got to experience the orphanage in the dark. Like so many others, they stuck around after the tour ended just to talk.

After that tour, the three began coming to Gettysburg more often, and we would always meet at Tommy's Pizza prior to them embarking on another one of my tours. Taking four different tours of mine, including the orphanage tour, Jennie Wade tour, Johnny Reb tour, and the haunted bus tour, the kids always enjoyed carrying some of my ghost hunting equipment, and went from being scared of the tours to big fans of them.

As I got to know Charles, I realized how much adversity he had overcome in his life and how deeply he loved his children. He always put their needs ahead of his own. And his children loved and adored him as well. I always had the utmost respect for Charles and continue to do so to this day.

One final note about him is that, being from Ohio, he is a die-hard Ohio State Buckeye fan. Since I attended Penn State University, I, of course, am a Nittany Lion fan, and bleed blue and white. The two of us would have a blast bantering back and forth about our respective teams. It was always good natured, and the mutual respect for each other was evident. The four of us always had a great time together and enjoyed each other's company.

Aaron was from central Pennsylvania and would come to Gettysburg numerous times every year. He would bring several of his friends with him, and they would take in one or more of my tours. Just like so many others I have already mentioned, the fun times did not end when the tours did. Some of our extracurricular activities included walking around the battlefield during the day, taking in various sites such as Devils Den, Little Round Top, and the Pennsylvania Monument. Of course, we journeyed out to the Sachs Covered Bridge several times. When we weren't out at the bridge, you could find us at O'Rourke's, enjoying a beer or more. I am proud to say that despite our age difference (me being double his age) he still could not outdrink me. I am certain our paths will cross again someday, and we can continue our talks about fishing and Penn State football.

On a Saturday evening during the summer of 2014, my life changed dramatically when I met a woman named Monica, and her daughter Felicia, who were from Allentown, Pennsylvania. The two were visiting Gettysburg and went on my haunted bus tour. I specifically remember the tour because it was one of the best tours I had ever conducted. All pistons were firing that night, and the sold-out crowd, including Monica and Felicia, had a blast. It just so happened to be my first non-Johnny Reb tour that I had received a standing ovation at the end.

Having enjoyed the bus tour, they decided to take my Johnny Reb tour the following evening. Johnny Reb had a great time picking on Felicia during the tour, and I was admittedly a little depressed when they left town. At the time I was not sure if I would ever see or hear from them again. Thankfully, it did not take long to realize they would become a major part of my life.

Gradually, Monica and I started texting each other, and eventually talking over the telephone. Monica was a kind, caring, generous, fun-loving, and intelligent woman. After getting to know each other via phone and text, she surprised me by showing up at a softball doubleheader that I coached. For her to drive that distance just to see me made me feel great, and I subsequently fell in love.

She would come and spend weekends at my house during the ghost tour season when Felicia was with her father. During the off season, I spent nearly every weekend at her house. I would take my daughter, and the two girls, who were similar ages, loved hanging out together.

I took Monica and Felicia to several Penn State football games, and they enjoyed coming up to my house for the weekend and exploring more of Gettysburg. Monica and I enjoyed each other's company, and we were growing closer by the day. At Christmas I went to Felicia's orchestra concert, and dance recital, while Monica would come and watch my daughter's softball games in the spring and summer.

Unfortunately, as often is the case, things did not work out between Monica and me (at no fault of hers). While we were together, however, it was such a wonderful time in my life, one that I will never forget. I wish Monica and Felicia nothing but true happiness wherever life takes them.

———◆———

Not only did I have the pleasure of meeting so many wonderful guests, but there was a tour guide I worked closely with that also had a profound effect on my life. Alexis G. was one of the funniest, most kind-hearted persons I have ever met. She was loyal beyond belief, and if she called you friend, you should consider yourself blessed. While all my fellow tour guides were incredible story tellers, Alexis took it to a whole new level. Not only did she portray the evil Rosa Carmichael in the Ghostly Encounter Orphanage tour, but she also depicted Mary Wade, Jennie's mother, in the Mary Wade Ghostly Encounter. Alexis and I formed an amazing bond and even created our own paranormal investigative team. We even had the opportunity once or twice to team up to do a tour, bringing our guests to their feet, but more on that later.

Alexis was also kind and generous enough to volunteer her time to go with me to Lancaster to help raise money for Tony F. She also accompanied me to a 150th anniversary celebration in Dover, a small town in York County, Pennsylvania, giving up an entire Saturday to help me. She is one of those people in life that you meet and never forget. It was my sincere honor and pleasure to work with someone so talented and dedicated as she was. Yes, she is one hell of an actress and storyteller, but an even better friend, and that is what makes her so special. If you are reading this Miss Alexis, I love and miss you, my friend.

———◆———

I also want to mention Duane and Elizabeth G, who were big fans of my ghost tours. They took nearly every different tour I offered. What makes them so special to me was they chose to get married in Gettysburg, on Halloween night, on Sachs Covered Bridge. And they invited me to attend. What an incredible honor that was. Not only was I there to witness two wonderful people exchanging their wedding vows, but my brother officiated the wedding.

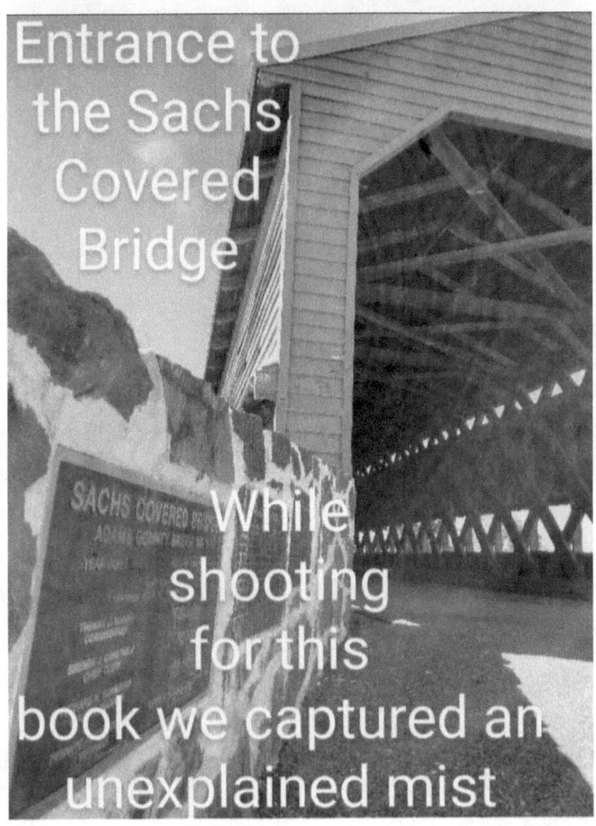

One incredible story that exemplifies how small the world we live in can be happened my last year of doing the tours. It concerned a man named Chris F. from Wyoming. During my years at Penn State back in the early 1990s, I met Chris, and we became instant friends. Not only did we live in the same dorm, but on the same floor. We had some great times on the fourth floor of Leete Hall in the Business and Society House in University Park.

Just like everything else in life, all good things come to an end, and that was the case with my college days. Once our days at Penn State were over, Chris and I went our separate ways, with him moving back out west. We lost contact with each other, and I figured I would never see my college friend again. (What were the chances of two individuals who lived thousands of miles apart ever seeing each other again?) Shockingly, our paths did cross once again on a Saturday night at the Sachs Covered Bridge.

During a haunted bus tour, our first stop was the bridge. After getting off the bus, the group and I walked onto the bridge itself, and I began my standard presentation. After giving a brief history of the bridge and telling a couple ghost stories, I cut the group loose to wander around and take some pictures. As I was minding my own business, this man, who was part of my bus tour, walked up to me and asked, "Do you remember me?"

People can change quite a bit over twenty-plus years, especially their appearance, so I did not recognize him. When he told me who he was, Chris from Wyoming, I was stunned. He recognized me because of my name tag. He and his family were in Gettysburg on vacation, decided to take a ghost tour, and as luck would have it, they chose the tour I was conducting. Was it fate, or did the mystique of the Sachs Covered Bridge bring two old friends back together?

<hr>

As I am sure many of you reading this book have done, I have visited our neighbor to the north (Canada) on several occasions. As a senior in high school, our band and chorus made a trip to Toronto. My second trip was when my wife (now ex) and I got married; we celebrated our honeymoon in Niagara Falls, particularly enjoying the helicopter ride over the falls. My third trip to Canada was a Labor Day mini vacation in which my wife and I took our daughter to see where her parents celebrated their honeymoon. What really stood out in my mind about the country was the hospitality of the local folks.

Jennifer B. her Aunt Peggy, and her Uncle Jim were from Canada and were annual visitors to Gettysburg. They were as polite and personable as the friendly Canadians I encountered on my trips there.

I fondly recall the first time I met the trio. I walked into our gift shop during my first year of doing the tours, and noticed this young lady, whom I had never met, walking toward me. She immediately started a conversation with me about ghosts, and I suppose she liked what I had to say because the three ended up taking my Jennie Wade Tour that evening. My initial conversation with Jen, and the subsequent tour, was the beginning of a longstanding friendship.

When they would make their annual trip to Gettysburg, they would always stay at the Artillery Ridge Campground, where they would invite me out to enjoy a nice relaxing night around the campfire. It was also not unusual for us to grab something to eat at Gettysburg Eddie's, or enjoy an ice cream at Mr. G's, only a block or two away from our gift shop.

An after-tour trip out to the Sach's Covered Bridge with Jen and her aunt and uncle would provide one of the most startling encounters I have ever witnessed, and left me in total awe. The encounter forever changed the way I allowed others to use my dowsing rods.

CHAPTER 8

WHAT DID SHE DO TO YOU?

One of my favorite spots in Gettysburg, and one which I have already mentioned several times in chapter 7, is the Sachs Covered Bridge. Except for the Jennie Wade House and orphanage, it is where I spent the most amount of time doing tours and investigations.

Every Saturday night from Memorial Day weekend through Halloween weekend, we would load up to forty guests for the Haunted Bus Tour. The main attraction, and what normally filled the bus, was the stop at the bridge. I was fortunate enough to be part of this tour for four years and loved every single time the bus fired up to take another group.

Imagine the anticipation as you are sitting, or in my case standing, on the bus on a Saturday evening, Halloween eve, as the bus begins its trek down Waterworks Road toward the bridge. The journey itself down the road was certainly not an easy one for the bus driver, who had to back the monstrosity of a bus up, navigating the hordes of other visitors already out there, as well as the dozens and dozens of vehicles lining both sides of the narrow road. And to further complicate the driver's task it was pitch dark by that time of night and, depending on the weather conditions, the windows could be completely fogged up.

As a direct result of our incredibly skilled drivers, there was not a single instance when we could not get back to the bridge. Excitement always filled the air as the passengers de-boarded, ready to check out the landmark, which was added to the National Register of Historic Places on August 25, 1980.

Not only did I spend time on the bridge as a guide and investigator, but I also took friends and family members to just hang out with me. It was not unusual for me to take my daughter and her friends, who would ice skate on Marsh Creek over the winter months. I was also able to take some of the most breathtaking pictures of the dam with the water flowing over, and the bridge in the background.

The bridge is not all about ghosts and spirits. The serenity and peacefulness of the flowing water is exhilarating. The tranquil atmosphere found out there today is totally opposite of what it was like in late June and early July of 1863. The structure, which is a Town truss wooden bridge, was constructed around 1854 by David S. Stone. It spans one hundred feet in length, and a little over fifteen feet wide. The cost to construct the bridge was $1,544, give or take.

Less than a decade after its completion, the bridge played an integral part in the Battle of Gettysburg. On July 1, 1863, two brigades of the First Corps of the Union Army crossed the bridge heading into Gettysburg. The Third Corps also crossed over it as they were heading toward the Black Horse Tavern.

During the three-day battle, the grounds surrounding the bridge were utilized as a Confederate field hospital, caring for the countless wounded soldiers. It was the ideal location because of the fresh water from the creek, and the abundant shade from the trees, which provided some much-welcomed relief during the sweltering hot July days.

With the end of the battle, a decisive and crucial Union victory, the Confederates were forced to retreat out of Gettysburg, and a majority of the Army of Northern Virginia, led by General Robert E. Lee, crossed back over the bridge, deflated and exhausted.

In 1938, the bridge was designated as Pennsylvania's most historic bridge by the Department of Highways, which later became the Pennsylvania Department of Transportation. On May 9, 1968, the landmark was closed to vehicular traffic for good, but continues to remain open to pedestrian traffic to this day.

The mere existence of the Sachs Covered Bridge was jeopardized on June 19, 1996, when torrential rain struck Cumberland and Freedom Townships, creating flash floods, and knocking the bridge off one of its abutments. Thankfully, due to generous financial support from some of the local businesses, the significant damage to the bridge was repaired, and the historical bridge was rededicated on July 21, 1997.

On any given summer night, dozens upon dozens of visitors can be seen meandering on the bridge and surrounding areas. Stories about hair-raising experiences are shared between paranormal enthusiasts, including one about a soldier hanging from the top of the roof's interior at one end of the bridge. Stories about continuous strong stenches of tobacco and gun powder, or even a body or two spotted in the creek, or hanging from the rafters. I truly believe there are merits to each story, but I was witness to one incident that left no doubt in my mind that spirits do occupy the bridge.

I mentioned in chapter 7 that Jen B, and her aunt and uncle were frequent guests on my tours. During one of their excursions to Gettysburg, and on their final night of vacation, they chose to take one last tour to hold them over until the following summer. After the tour concluded, we hopped in my car, and I drove them out to the bridge. They had never been to the bridge, or even heard of it.

They were just as interested in the unrivaled history of the town as they were with the unexplained, so I indulged them with a brief background of the bridge, which they were fascinated by. I then retrieved the divining rods from my bag. The rods were always one of my favorite tools to use during an investigation, often being utilized to communicate with the spirits.

I have always had legitimate safety concerns, about being attacked by a spirit, from using the rods, so before going any further, I said my customary prayer, asking for protection while I used them. With that out of the way, I began using the rods, and had very little responses.

Several minutes elapsed without any significant action, so I went to put them back in my bag. I was convinced the spirits simply did not want to communicate that evening. Before I had the chance to put them away, however, Jen asked if she could try them. Normally I would say no, but her aunt and uncle both insisted she would be fine, so I reluctantly handed them to her.

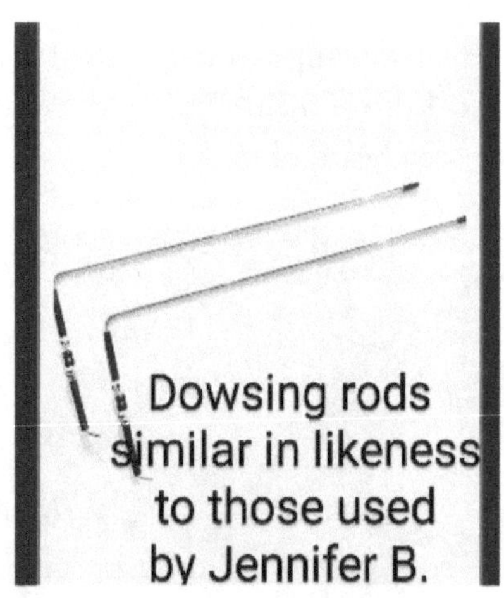

To her delight, as soon as she started asking questions, there was action with the rods. Her excitement did not last long, however. Within a minute or two I noticed she was having difficulty speaking. It got to the point she could barely utter a word, so I asked her if she was okay. Nodding her head up and down, she continued to ask questions while struggling to get her words out.

As the seconds turned to minutes, not only was her speech getting worse, but I noticed her breathing was labored. Realizing the situation was quickly getting out of control, I grabbed the rods, taking them from her. I immediately took her by the arm and escorted her off the bridge.

Once the four of us were off the bridge, despite the tears streaming down her cheeks and the look of total despair and disbelief across her face, she gradually started to once again breathe normally. After a few minutes, once Jim, Peggy, and I were able to get her calmed down, she wanted to go back on the bridge. The three of us quickly put a stop to that idea.

Climbing back into my car, she told me it felt like someone had their hands clasped around her throat, choking her. And the longer she held the divining rods, the tighter the grip around her throat got. When I took the rods from her, the grip loosened, and by the time we were off the bridge, the grip was completely gone and she was able to breathe again.

As soon as we were on the main road heading back into town, she started complaining that her throat hurt and she was having trouble swallowing, so I pulled my car over. "It's nothing serious," she explained. "It reminds me of when I had strep throat." When I turned the interior light on, I noticed red marks, like a set of fingerprints, around her neck. Her neck was bruised, and it definitely did not look like that prior to the divining rods incident.

By the time we got back into town, Jen was back to her happy, bubbly self, while the rest of us were still in a state of pure shock. Before they got into their car to return to their campground, Jen asked me what I thought happened to her. As straightforward as I could possibly be, I answered her, "I have no idea."

After that night, my whole approach changed concerning whom I allowed to use the divining rods. I no longer permitted anyone under the age of eighteen to use them, and for guests over eighteen who wanted to use them, I strongly encouraged them to say a prayer of protection, no matter what their religious beliefs were. Thankfully, most people witnessed me saying a prayer before using them, and followed in my footsteps.

My three Canadian friends went back home with a great story to tell, and with their permission, I added Jen's experience to my bus tour, reciting it to my guests as we were leaving the bridge. Jen, Peggy, and Jim returned every year, and we would make a special trip out to the historical bridge, but despite Jen's urging, I never took the divining rods with me.

None of us know why the spirits turned on Jen that night. Nobody knows why they manifest themselves to some, but not others. Do they target certain individuals, and if so, why? Were the spirits angry at her for some reason? Perhaps she reminded them of someone they once knew. Furthermore, why did the spirits appease me that night in the Jennie Wade House when the chamber pot slid several feet across the floor (see chapter 3) after ignoring the investigators for over an hour? Unfortunately, these are questions that we will never know the answer to, but nevertheless, we remain intrigued by the phenomenon.

The mystery of spirit activity intensified for me late one evening on my way home from the tour center and got even more bizarre as the night turned into morning. It did not happen close to home; it happened at home.

CHAPTER 9

STAY AWAY FROM MY HOUSE, THANK YOU VERY MUCH

Anyone who knows me knows how regimented I am. No matter where I find myself, whether it is work, home, vacation, coaching basketball or softball, or visiting friends, I have a routine. I am not a fan of change. Once I get into a safe, comfortable routine, I try to follow it as much as possible.

Despite my strong desire to maintain the status quo, I am, however, able to adapt to change when necessary. If I am doing something that just does not seem right, I am smart enough to realize a change may be warranted, and I will not hesitate to make one. I may seem irritable at first, but once I get comfortable, the sky is the limit.

Why do I mention my affinity for a systematic routine? It has a lot to do with an experience I am about to share with you, one that demonstrated a strong need for a change in my system, for the sake of my own sanity.

As mentioned previously, I kept myself extremely busy, especially during the summer months. I worked a full-time job as a general manager for a towing and repossession company, working in excess of forty hours per week. It was a high-paced, highly stressful job in which I was responsible for payroll, accounts payable and receivable, scheduling, legal compliance, and customer service. There was very little, if any, down time with that job.

Every afternoon, once I would leave that job, I would go home for an hour or two and attempt to decompress before doing at least one tour. Some nights it would be midnight, or later, until I got home. Once home,

I would grab a couple hours of sleep before starting the process all over again. Thankfully I had the weekends to sleep in, until spring and summer softball began.

One of the craziest stretches of my life occurred in July 2013. Since July was, by far, the busiest month of the summer, I had done tours every night for three straight weeks. As I was wrapping up that crazy schedule, I had a mid-week ghost tour doubleheader. My first tour of the evening was in the orphanage, and I finished out the night with a sold-out tour in the Jennie Wade House. While nothing out of the ordinary happened during either tour, it was a great night with the guests having an enjoyable time.

Before heading home, I stuck around the Jennie Wade House and showed some pictures after the tour. It was shortly after midnight when I finally climbed in my car and left. After passing through the craziness of what is known as the Gettysburg square, I headed east on Route 30. As I passed the Dairy Queen on my right-hand side, I heard voices coming from my back seat. Startled, I pulled my car over, and realized the digital recorder I had in my bag of investigating equipment was playing.

My bag of equipment consisted of hundreds of dollars' worth of ghost hunting equipment such as voice recorders, K2 meters, divining rods, a camera, and so forth. I immediately turned the digital recorder off and continued the drive home.

As part of my routine, I stopped at Sheetz to fill up my thirty-two-ounce travel mug with Diet Cherry Pepsi from the fountain. It was not unusual for me to sweat off a few pounds during my tours, so I would replenish myself. Following that brief stop, I got on Route 15 North for the final 20-minute stretch of my drive home.

About five minutes after getting on Route 15, my digital recorder once again started playing. It was playing a portion of a previous investigation I had conducted. For the remainder of my drive home, all I heard was my voice asking questions, trying to elicit a response of some sort. While it was weird hearing the digital recorder playing, I chalked it up as a coincidence that it happened twice on my drive home.

When I arrived home and took the bag of equipment into my house, the digital recorder was still playing. What really caught my attention was the fact that the lights on my K2 meter were lit up like a Christmas tree.

I was somewhat perplexed with the meter being on because I specifically remembered checking it to make sure it was off prior to leaving the tour center parking lot. I always make it a habit (a "routine") of double checking to make sure all of the equipment is off because the K2 meter itself takes a 9-volt battery, which is not cheap. I eventually decided that I may have bumped the on/off button when I put it in my bag.

Before even walking into my living room, I once again turned the digital recorder and K2 meter off. I also checked the remainder of my equipment to make sure they were off as well. I subsequently placed the bag on my dining room table, as I always did when I got home. By that time it was close to one in the morning, so I was ready to settle in for the night.

During and after the tours, my adrenaline was always through the roof, which made it nearly impossible to go right to sleep. This night was no different. I am not sure if it was because of what happened with the recorder and the meter, or if I was preoccupied with the thoughts of an extremely important meeting I had with one of my company's major accounts in just a few hours, but it took me a little longer than usual to fall asleep. Like I always did when I could not fall asleep, I watched some television.

Despite only getting about three hours of sleep, I got up at five-thirty and hopped into the shower. At quarter after six, I emerged from my bedroom, but stopped dead in my tracks when I noticed my ghost hunting equipment and empty bag strewn across the floor in my hallway.

Stunned, my first concern was somebody had broken into my house. Prior to falling asleep I had been awake for over twenty hours, and when I finally did fall asleep, I was in such a deep sleep that perhaps I had slept through an intrusion. As I looked around, however, I realized nothing else was askew, and nothing was missing.

Picking up everything off the floor, I tried to figure out how my bag of equipment went from the dining room table, through the kitchen, through the living room, and back into the hallway leading into my bedroom.

My daughter was at her mother's house, and the only pets I had at the time were David and Goliath, my two goldfish. Even an earthquake would not have caused the bag full of equipment to go from the dining room table to the hallway.

Astonished at what had taken place, I ended up being about fifteen minutes late for work, which was inconsequential since I was the general manager, and the meeting did not start until mid-morning. However, being late was extremely unusual for me. That day at work, and more specifically the meeting, was unproductive. I was there in body, but not in spirit. All I could do was think about what had happened in my home the previous night.

Arriving early for my tour that evening, I explained to another one of the tour guides what had happened from the minute I left the tour center until I woke up earlier that morning. To my surprise, she asked me something I never even gave a thought to: before leaving the parking lot, did I tell the spirits to stay in Gettysburg, and not follow me home?

When she said it, I initially thought the notion sounded absurd, but the more I thought about it, the more I considered it. I figured no harm could be done by trying it. After my tour that evening, and before starting up my car, I told the spirits I enjoyed talking to them, and I promised to return soon to do it again, but I was leaving, and they had to stay where they were, in Gettysburg.

Thankfully, I had a peaceful and uneventful night's sleep, so I said the same thing the following night before heading home. This speech I made before climbing into my car became part of my routine. Whether the speech I gave helped keep the spirits in Gettysburg I will never know, but I never again had an experience like I did that night in my house. If nothing else, I am sure I brought some amusement to people walking or driving by when they noticed this middle-aged man talking to himself.

So, what really happened that night? How did my ghost hunting equipment, which was inside a bag, get from the dining room table to the hallway outside my door on the opposite end of my house? Did I sleepwalk (something I had never done before), grab my bag off the table, walk back the hallway, and dump the equipment all over the floor before crawling back into bed? Alternatively, did someone or something not of this world accompany me home that night? I may never know the truth, but I have my opinion, and after reading this chapter, hopefully you have yours as well.

CHAPTER 10

MARY ANN WADE VERSUS JOHNNY REB

This book, *Paranormal Experiences as Told by a Gettysburg Ghost Tour Guide*, is more than just a memoir, a recounting of paranormal experiences I had, guests had, or we shared together. According to *Webster's New World Dictionary and Thesaurus*, Second Edition, the definition of memoir is, "a record of events based on the writer's personal knowledge." While many of the chapters herein are dedicated to unexplained experiences, there were other amazing times that made an impression on me, including the following one, which I am proud and honored to share with you.

Alexis G., in my opinion, is the greatest storyteller I have ever met or had the luxury of being around. I could listen to her for hours and be mesmerized. The way she could capture her audience's attention was awe inspiring. I always strived to be as good as she was, even though I know that was just not possible.

The first time I met her was in the Jennie Wade House. There were approximately forty of us that responded to the add in the newspaper asking for ghost tour guides, and we all got together for a walkthrough of the house before we auditioned for the part. As part of the walkthrough, we were told a couple of the stories that were used during the tours themselves. Alexis was the guide who narrated that evening, and she made one hell of a first impression on me. She did not just tell a story, she really got into it. Her delivery was phenomenal, and her enthusiasm was second to none. When I left the Jennie Wade House that evening, I was excited, but also intimidated. Would I ever be able to lead a tour like she did if I got the job?

Following a first and second audition, I was thrilled to get the job. Alexis and I started talking more and more, and quickly became good friends. We made it a point whenever we had tours on the same night to meet early at Subway for a soda, a cookie or two, and (best of all) heartfelt conversation.

As the years progressed, so did our friendship. It was not unusual for the two of us to proudly represent our tour company by attending and participating in various charitable events and celebrations. She always had a kind word to offer and could turn a bad day into a happy one.

Occasionally, we would enjoy a dinner at O'Rourke's. I fondly recall celebrating her sixtieth birthday over dinner there prior to a tour. During the off season, Alexis and her husband were kind enough to invite me to their beautiful home for pizza, and so she could proudly show off her cats.

We formed our own paranormal investigative team, using the equipment we had purchased throughout the years. The reasons we formed our own team were twofold. First, we enjoyed investigating, and second, we loved laughing and having fun. The last things on our mind during the investigation were making money or being on television.

There was no lack of humorous moments we had together either. All the tour guides knew Alexis was scared of all thing's ghostly, so of course we took every opportunity to play off of that. During my first year, the tour guide conducting the Jennie Wade midnight tour on Saturday nights was responsible for turning off lights in the Jennie Wade gift shop before leaving. By midnight, the gift shop had been closed for several hours, and it was very dark, and quiet, inside.

One Saturday night I knew she would be going into the gift shop, so I hid behind the counter and waited for her arrival. At midnight, like clockwork, she used her key to unlock the door and came sauntering in to turn the lights out. When I jumped out at her, she screamed so loud the guests inside the house itself heard her. At first, I was concerned she may have had a heart attack, but other than being scared half to death, thankfully she was just fine.

On another occasion, I was down in the cellar of the house, in the dark, and she came walking down to turn the lights on. When she saw me standing there, she was so scared she twirled around, and ran up the cellar steps. Afraid she would run right onto Baltimore Street and get hit by a car, I had to chase her down and show her it was just me.

In my opinion, the most hilarious incident with Alexis happened in the hallway leading back to the pit area in the cellar of the orphanage. Before our tours began that evening, she and I wanted to do some investigating, so I followed her down the steps. When we got to the opening of the dungeon, she peered in, and as she did, a man's voice could be heard calling out, "Alexis, Alexis." I started laughing because I instantly recognized the voice of our manager, who was simply playing a joke on us. Alexis apparently did not know it was him.

She looked at me in stark terror. She reached into her pocket, grabbed her lighter, lit it (the lights in the hallway were out so it was very dark), and came charging toward me as I was standing between her and the exit out of the hallway. Quickly getting out of her way so I didn't get run over, or set on fire, I watched her sprint down the hallway and, just like that, she was out of the cellar.

The one thing that struck me most was how Alexis would never get angry (at least she never showed it) at the lighthearted practical jokes we subjected her to. Not only did she not get angry, but she laughed right along with us. Alexis took it all in stride.

Professionally, we had the utmost respect for each other. I would often do the introductions for her Rosa Carmichael Ghostly Encounter tours which began back in the courtyard. Her guests loved it when I would talk smack about the sinister matron only to have her suddenly appear and literally chase me away. It made a great first impression.

On occasion, we would step in and participate in each other's tour. This was also a favorite of our guests. The way we played off each other was fantastic. The chemistry between us was second to none, and the guests could sense that.

On the weekends during the summer months, it was rare when we did not work together on the same midnight tours. I would play my Johnny Reb character, and she would be in the cellar leading the investigative portion of the tour, or alternately, she was Mrs. Wade, Jennie's mother, and I was in the cellar. We even participated in the holiday tour together; she was Mrs. Wade and I was a Union soldier helping the family get to safety.

So why did we work so well together? The answer is simple. We were both extremely popular tour guides, but instead of competing against each other, we supported each other, rooting for the other to succeed. Playing off each other just made us stronger as we somehow knew what the other was thinking. We worked together like a well-oiled machine, and our cohesiveness was never more obvious than on a spring night in 2015.

Our tour company was always busy during the months of March, April, and May due to private group tours consisting of school students and chaperones from across the United States who had come to Gettysburg. On that particular spring evening there was a group of junior high school students from New York doing a Jennie Wade tour.

Alexis and I both had a group tour, but one of the groups never showed up, so on the spur of the moment, we decided to get together and give those kids a tour they would never forget. As it turned out, it was a tour none of us would ever forget.

Fortunately, both of us had our Ghostly Encounter tour outfits with us, Alexis with her Mary Ann Felby Wade, and me with Johnny Reb. It did not take us long to change into our respective outfits and become each other's nemesis.

For the joint venture, we focused on the sad events of July 3, 1863, involving the death of Jennie at the hands of a Confederate soldier. What made the death even more devastating was the fact that Jennie's mother was several feet away from her daughter when she was accidently killed. The discovery of her daughter's lifeless body prompted Mrs. Wade to return to the parlor where the rest of the family was, and quietly announce, "Georgia, your sister is dead."

Absolute horror and pure fear must have overcome the surviving family members. Jennie lay dead on the floor; bullets were spraying all around her family, including where one-week-old Louis, Georgia's newborn, was located. Mrs. Wade had to immediately put her devastation and mourning aside, and make sure the remainder of the family, who were still alive, remained safe. Finally, once they reached a place of apparent safety, she had to sit mere feet away from her beloved daughter's dead body while the remainder of the battle played out all around them.

What were Mrs. Wade's thoughts during the twenty-four plus hours they remained in the cellar? It is almost certain she questioned how something that tragic could happen. I am sure she asked over and over again who would shoot her daughter, and why. While we don't know exactly who fired the bullet, it is believed to have come from a Confederate soldier with one of the Louisiana Infantry companies.

The fighting Louisiana Tigers, as they were referred to because of their tenacity, were positioned in the southern part of the borough of Gettysburg, on both sides of Baltimore Street. Their adversaries were located on East Cemetery Hill. Constant skirmishes between the two sides flooded the aforesaid Baltimore Street with bullets, placing Georgia's home (where the family was staying) right in the middle.

After analyzing the bullet hole in the north door, including the position and angle, as well as the direction the bullet came from, it is believed the bullet, while inadvertent, was, in fact, fired by one of the Louisiana Tigers' sharpshooters. It was because of that belief that I created Johnny Reb, the fictitious, unknown soldier who was filled with guilt, anger, and sadness.

Fast forward nearly one hundred fifty-two years later (the time of the group tour), and we find Mrs. Wade and Johnny Reb sparring verbally in front of a group of New York school students. During the seventy-five-minute tour, Mrs. Wade, just like everyone else, blamed Johnny Reb for her daughter's death. Johnny, of course, vehemently disagreed with Mrs. Wade's accusations. After leading the group of youngsters through the entire house, Alexis and I asked the group, "Did Johnny Reb fire the bullet?" As usual, most of them answered yes. Mary Wade's argument prevailed, while Johnny Reb's fell short, but on that evening, there were no losers.

What made the tour that evening so special? Why did Alexis and I receive a prolonged standing ovation, and pleas for more? I believe there were several reasons. First, incredibly both of us improvised the entire time. Our dialogue was not rehearsed, or even discussed beforehand. At that point, we both knew each other's characters and their history and had played our own characters so often, that we just took it and ran.

Second, our dialogue was a mixture of anger, sadness, guilt, resentment, and even some humor. Mary Wade presented her case, amidst constant interruption and contrariness from Johnny Reb, and Johnny presented his case, encountering the same barrage of insults and disagreements levied by Mrs. Wade.

Finally, the children and chaperones were entranced by what was happening, hanging on our every word and action. While true performers give it their all every time out, and anybody who has ever taken either of our tours would tell you we did, it is also true that we as performers are energized by positive guest reactions during our presentation, which we most definitely had that night.

Despite our hopes to do so, our stars never aligned again, and we were never able to perform a joint tour together after that night. Getting together again would have been something truly memorable, much like what happened on October 9, 2010.

CHAPTER 11

OCTOBER 9, 2010

"What is a Medium?" I was often asked that question during my tours. Guests would also ask me what my thoughts were on that subject. The first question I had no problem answering. A medium is one through whom messages are supposedly sent from the dead. The second question was more difficult for me to answer, at least for the first several months of my tour guide career.

Before my tour guide career, I had a bad experience with a psychic which made me skeptical of the entire concept. My ex-wife, who was gullible to a fault (she once sent two thousand dollars via Western Union to a supposed Spanish lottery processing center because she was told she won a Spanish lottery), sought the expertise of a psychic on the boardwalk in Atlantic City, New Jersey. Unbeknownst to me (I was struggling at the blackjack table in the Wild Wild West Casino), she paid twenty dollars for a reading. Then she was talked into paying another forty dollars for an "extended" reading. By the time I met back up with her, she had dished out over two hundred dollars. Since I had just lost miserably in the casino, I could not really say too much, but the experience left a terrible taste in my mouth for the whole psychic idea.

My skepticism did not last long, however. The first two years I was a tour guide, our company employed a psychic medium for the Friday night midnight tour in the orphanage, as well as the Saturday night midnight tour through the Jennie Wade house.

The first midnight tour I ever conducted was in the Jennie Wade house. As was always the case, the medium was in the cellar when I took my group down the steps where Jennie's dead body had at one time laid. Jennie was surrounded in that cellar by her family, until the bloody battle ended. Before the guests had a chance to sit down, the medium singled out a middle-aged woman who was with her husband. He told the guest where she could find her mother's ring.

Bursting into tears, the woman was astonished at what she had just heard. She explained to the group that her mother had just passed away suddenly and unexpectedly, and her ring, which had major sentimental significance, had gone missing. Despite an exhaustive search of her late mother's residence, the ring could not be located.

Still in a state of total disbelief because she had never spoken with, or even met, our medium, she quickly began asking questions, and it was revealed that her mother had just disclosed the location of the missing ring to him, and urged him to pass it on to her daughter.

The midnight tour concluded at approximately one fifteen in the morning, and when I woke up the following morning, there was a lengthy, heartfelt email from the female guest. She indicated that the ring had meant so much to her, she and her husband had cut their weekend getaway short and driven straight to her mother's residence, where she found the ring precisely where the medium had told her to look. She was incredibly grateful. This event changed my whole attitude about psychic mediums. From that point on, I was a believer.

Throughout the spring and summer of 2010, the medium and I became close friends. The more I talked to him, the more I knew he was the real deal. He was genuine, truthful, and sincere. If there was nothing going on in the building that night as far as spirit activity, he would not hesitate to tell the guests just that. Yes, he even helped me out with some unanswered questions, feelings, and emotions that were plaguing me. Unlike the faux psychic on the Atlantic City boardwalk that bamboozled my ex-wife, he never asked for a penny in return.

As the summer of 2010 turned to fall, I was doing the midnight tours through the Jennie Wade house nearly every Saturday night, and was consistently impressed with what this medium had to say. I was also impressed with how quickly he could get the guests' attention. When he spoke, everyone listened.

When October arrived, there was less than two months remaining in my inaugural season of conducting the ghost tours. October is Halloween season, and the ghost tour company was crazy busy, especially during the weekends. It was not unusual for our weekend tours in October to be sold out, and unlike other tour companies in town who herded guests like cattle, we limited our tours to a maximum of twenty-five people.

Saturday, October 9, 2010, was like any other Saturday in early Autumn. The weather was beautiful. The ninety-degree days of summer were in the rear-view mirror, and the freezing cold temperatures had not yet arrived. The town at that time of year is breathtaking with the leaves changing colors and Halloween decorations taking over.

Gettysburg was quite crowded that Saturday night, as most motels displayed their "no vacancy" signs due to it being Columbus Day weekend. It was the final chance for people to sneak in an extra weekend day before the cold weather and holiday season rolled in.

A brisk chill could be felt that evening as we started our tours, but the stars were shining beautifully, illuminating the otherwise dark sky. Just a couple of weeks before Halloween, we were gearing up for an extremely busy night, and we were not disappointed.

It was still a year or so before I started doing the Haunted Bus tour, but I still had two tours in the Jennie Wade house that night, including the third tour during the midnight tour. Because of its popularity, our Saturday night midnight tours were broken down into three groups. The reason it was called the midnight tour was all three groups were inside the house at midnight when the lights were turned out.

Since the entire tour took place inside the house, we had to stagger our start times in order to avoid an over-crowded mess. The first group started their tour at ten forty-five, which placed them in the cellar with the medium at midnight. The second group began thirty minutes later, at eleven fifteen, placing them on the second floor at midnight, and the third and final group began their tour at eleven thirty-five, which meant the group was in the kitchen and parlor area at midnight. I always remained with my group, so I was in the kitchen with them at midnight when the lights were turned off.

When the lights came back on about five minutes after midnight, group one's tour concluded, and group two proceeded to the cellar for the medium's presentation, while my group toured the rest of the house, including both the McClelland and McClain sides of the house. It was essential that all three guides followed the timeline in order to successfully afford each group ample time in each of the locations within the house and cellar.

At twelve forty, once group two was finished in the cellar, I escorted my group down the steps. After assuming my usual position opposite the medium in the back of the cellar, I handed the presentation over to him. For what was supposed to be the next half hour, I sat in the back, and took in what the medium had to say.

As soon as he began his presentation, I noticed something was amiss with him. I had spoken to him when I first walked my group down the steps just minutes before, and he seemed his normal self, but now there was definitely something wrong. On several occasions, he stopped talking in mid-sentence, and stared into space, like he was in a trance.

Swaying back and forth, he turned and looked toward the corner in which the wooden water trough, which was utilized during the battle to supply water for the horses, was located. After about two minutes of exhibiting this same behavior, I became concerned that there was something medically wrong with him, so I asked him if everything was okay. Holding up his hand to silence me, he continued staring into the corner for an additional minute or so.

Finally breaking the silence, he shifted his attention to me, asking me if I recognized the name Mary. Confused as to what was happening, I asked the group if anybody's name was Mary. He immediately corrected me, telling me it was not a guest, but was, in fact, associated somehow with the house.

Repeating the name Mary several times, it finally clicked with me that there were two Mary's linked to the house. Mary Ann Wade, Jennie's mother, and Mary Virginia Wade, Jennie herself. I failed to associate the name Mary with Jennie at first because Jennie's birth name was Mary Virginia, and it was not until a local newspaper erroneously identified her as Jennie, that she became commonly referred to a Jennie, even though her real name was Mary.

Informing the medium of the two possibilities, he instantly replied, "She said her nickname is Gin." Gin, because of her middle name, Virginia, was the nickname she often used. Not only was I astonished, but the guests were hanging on every word the medium was saying. We quickly realized we were witnessing something truly special.

He explained how she was showing him pictures of various people she knew, and asking if he knew where they were, or what happened to them. While this was taking place, I instructed the group to snap a lot of pictures, especially in the corner the medium was staring into.

At approximately twenty minutes after one, the vibrating alarm on my phone went off, signaling the end of the tour. The medium, however, continued his dialogue with Jennie, so with his permission, I gave our guests an option: I would open the cellar door, and people could either leave or they could stick around for a few more minutes until he was done. Surprisingly, not a single guest chose to leave.

It was my experience that if the tours lasted too long, we would sometimes get complaints. Guests would get impatient, wanting to get back to their motel rooms, campsites, or homes after a long, tiresome day of touring the battlefield. I understood their positions, which is why I afforded them the opportunity to leave if they wanted to.

At that point, my plan was to continue for ten or fifteen more minutes, and end the tour at that point. The group and I were enthralled by what was taking place, and I certainly did not want to end their good time. I saw what was going on as a once-in-a-lifetime experience for the guests, but in the same sense, I could not allow it to go on all night.

Waiting for what I thought was about fifteen minutes, I looked at my watch, and to my shock, it was approaching three thirty in the morning. When I announced we had to end the tour, the guests were not happy. They wanted it to continue, but when I informed them what time it was, they thought I was lying. Several guests insisted there was no way we were down in that cellar for nearly three hours. In talking with some of the guests as they were leaving, they all agreed that it seemed like, for a period of time, we were in our own little world down in the cellar.

An additional twenty minutes elapsed before I was finally able to clear the cellar. One of the final guests to leave was a gentleman in his mid forties. He approached me and told me that the only reason he had signed up for the tour was because his fiancé insisted he join her. He told me that prior to the tour that evening, he thought the whole ghost tour thing was a hoax, but reluctantly agreed to go to make her happy. After what had happened, he informed me his whole attitude had changed. He was now a believer and thanked me for the "outstanding" tour. Even at three forty-five in the morning, I could sense the excitement and enthusiasm in that man's voice.

Later that Sunday evening, I received an email from that man and his fiancé. They thanked me once again for the tour. The email also contained an attachment, which was a picture she had taken, showing a heavy mist in the corner that the medium was staring into. Was it Jennie Wade? The psychic medium said it was, and I believe him.

I began this chapter with a question tour guests routinely asked me, and I will finish the chapter with another one: What was the most unusual experience I encountered while doing tours? I can answer that without a doubt, what occurred on the evening of Saturday, October 9, 2010, and the early hours of Sunday, October 10, 2010, which included the two-hour gap of time nobody could account for, was the most unusual, but there were so many others.

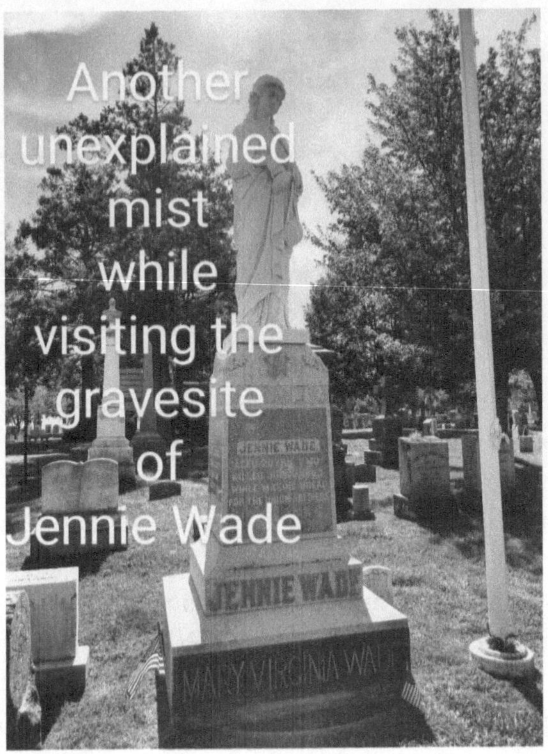

CHAPTER 12

WHAT ARE YOU LOOKING AT?

"But if you don't coach our team, we can't play. Nobody else wants to," my oldest niece pleaded with me. She was in sixth grade, and I was in my twenties working a full-time job at a local law firm as a paralegal.

"Tiff, you don't understand, I don't know enough about basketball to teach it to kids," I answered, telling her the truth. Out of the three most popular sports shown on television (football, basketball, and baseball), basketball was the sport I knew the least about.

Unable to deny my niece and other fifth and sixth graders the opportunity to play, I reluctantly agreed. I did not know it at the time, but coaching would become my second greatest passion next to being a ghost tour guide.

In my fifteenth year of coaching basketball, first for my niece's teams, and then for my daughter's, my daughter decided she also wanted to play softball. Since I had plenty of experience coaching youth sports, I was asked by the softball association to help out with her team. I was still coaching basketball, had my full-time job, and telling ghost stories part time, so I had my plate full, but I figured helping out would not take too much of my time.

Before even stepping on the softball diamond to "help out," I was somehow named the head coach. As the basketball season was still in full swing, softball practices started. What resulted was one unbelievably chaotic schedule on my part with two jobs and spending four nights a week coaching two sports (not to mention the basketball games every weekend).

Mercifully the basketball season ended in March every year, just prior to the ghost tour season really ramping up, and never started back up until November, when the tour season was winding down. Softball, however, started the beginning of March with spring ball, and finished at the end of October with fall ball. Because of my hectic schedule, there were weeks I did not know if I was coming or going, but I thoroughly enjoyed every minute of coaching.

Coaching softball for three years, I finally felt like I knew what I was doing. My teams never had the most talent, in fact far from it, but they always played their hearts out, which, in my opinion, was more important at their age. In my first year of coaching softball, we won the championship after starting the season with five straight losses. My final two years found us losing in the championship game both years.

During my third year of coaching softball, I became romantically involved, and after careful consideration, I decided to make my third year the last. It was a very difficult decision, but trying to balance two jobs, coaching, and spending time developing a relationship, was taking its toll on me. I can honestly say that I don't know too many coaches who coached a basketball team, while at the same time coaching their rival school's softball team. Yes, my daughter played in both . . . only in youth league.

In the middle of my second year of coaching softball, I had an orphanage tour on a Friday night. The tour went extremely well, but nothing extraordinary happened, or so I thought. At the time I believed it to be just another great orphanage tour, but I would soon find out it was anything but ordinary.

My team had a ten o'clock softball game the next morning. I arrived at the field two hours prior to our game starting like I normally would. I always left my cell phone in my car during games for two reasons; first, I did not want to be coaching third base and have my phone go off, and second, the players had a habit of grabbing my phone when I was not paying attention and doing crazy things such as snapping dozens of selfies or setting the alarm for three o'clock in the morning. I figured it was a Saturday morning and my daughter was with me, so anyone that needed to talk to me could wait until after the game.

The game ended around noon, so I was without my phone for about four hours. After loading the equipment bag into my car, I checked my phone, and could not believe what I saw. I had over twenty missed calls, and six voice messages.

Panic set it, briefly. I could not understand who was trying to reach me that many times. The calls came from the same number, so I figured something important was happening. Once I realized that it was the tour company trying to reach me, I felt somewhat better. The six voice messages all said the same thing: "Call me as soon as you get this message!"

Before I took my daughter to McDonalds for lunch, I called the gift shop. The first several times I called the line was busy, but I did not stop trying. The telephone was normally busy Saturday mornings, so I said to my daughter, "I wonder what's going on?" She suggested they needed me to do another tour that night, which happened frequently, but I quickly dismissed that notion because normally it was my manager who called me, and not the cashier at the gift shop. Furthermore, he would call me once, and if I did not answer, he would leave a message for me to call him back. He never called me twenty times.

With each unsuccessful attempt to reach someone in the gift shop, I grew more impatient. I thought something was terribly wrong (I am a pessimist by nature). A million different possibilities raced through my mind. I knew the gift shop received a large quantity of calls on Saturday mornings by guests who wanted to reserve their spots on the tours that evening, but I wanted to know what was so important that warranted over twenty telephone calls, and a half dozen voice messages.

Finally, after what seemed like an eternity, but in all actuality was only several minutes, the gift shop employee answered the telephone. When she realized it was me calling her back, she practically scolded me, like a parent scolds a child, for not answering my phone. Her voice had a feverish tone to it, and I could tell she was beside herself to tell me something.

She proceeded to explain that when she arrived at the gift shop at ten, two women were standing at the door waiting for her. They had taken my orphanage tour the night before. They informed her that they had taken my advice and continuously snapped pictures throughout the entire tour. Once they got back to their motel room, they reviewed the photos they had taken and were amazed at what they saw in one of them.

The first room tours stopped at once inside the building was referred to as the Legends and Showcase room. Inside that room is a short animatronics presentation of some of the events that happened in or around Gettysburg, not only during the battle, but before and after as well. The primary emphasis of that room was on the unexplained and paranormal activity. More importantly, however, was that the first room was the dining room during the era in which the orphanage was open.

In that room, I would explain to guests what had happened there in the past. This was the same room in which little Bertie Leonard from New Bedford, Massachusetts, sat and ate her meals. Her father, having unselfishly and heroically fought and lost his life for the Massachusetts Forty-Seventh infantry, leaving her an orphan at two years old. The child dutifully sits at the dining table listening to the blessing as it was given prior to each and every meal she ate. Those were the good times at the orphanage.

And then there was Bella Hunter, an infant when her father signed up with the Pennsylvania Heavy Artillery, who sadly became yet another helpless orphan at five years of age after her beloved father had returned from war as a severely bruised and broken man, eventually succumbing to horrible health and disease. Bella, like so many other innocent children, was neglected due to her father's inability to properly care for her to the fullest extent until the orphanage opened its doors, welcoming her with open arms and giving her a very much needed second chance in life.

Bella waits patiently at the dining room table, her mouthwatering, anticipating the Christmas feast she is about to enjoy. She has transformed from the timid and fragile girl when she first arrived, to strong and healthy under Philinda Humiston's guidance. Sadly, she would later fall victim to Rosa Carmichael's horrific torture and abuse, and would sit in this same dining room years later, miserable and broken-hearted, remembering and yearning for the good times to return.

The dining room, like so many other rooms inside that building, a building which was used as the headquarters for Union Major General Oliver O. Howard, played witness to the best of times, when the children were happy and healthy, and the worst of times, when the children were starved, beaten, and most likely killed.

I was giving my presentation to the guests inside that dining room, while many of them were busy snapping pictures. While they wanted to hear what I had to say (at least, I would like to think they did), they also wanted to capture something, anything, to make their experience on the ghost tour unforgettable, and there was no better place to do just that than the dining room, a room in which investigators fall all over themselves to investigate.

Ardently snapping picture after picture in that room during my presentation were the two women who were waiting at the gift shop door when it opened. In one of the several dozen pictures they took, I was standing in front talking, and just feet away from me was a woman's face glaring at me. The unidentified older woman had a scowl on her face. If looks could have killed, I would have immediately found myself six feet under.

The cashier at the gift shop told me all of this so rapidly and excitedly, that I was barely able to understand her, and had to ask her to slow down a bit. Along with her, I could also hear the two women in the background, insisting there was no woman there when they snapped the pictures, and they were correct: at no point was there an older woman, or any woman for that matter, standing beside me during my presentation.

Please don't get me wrong, I absolutely love the excitement guests often exhibited when describing their pictures to me, believing they captured the ultimate image, proving once and for all ghosts and spirits really do exist. Unfortunately, while they usually did capture something unique and interesting, normally there was an explanation behind it. There are exceptions, but they were few, and I assumed this picture was not one of the exceptions.

Despite our gift shop employee's obstinacy that I come right up to check out the picture, I was with my daughter, and my time with her on the weekends was already limited. The cashier did take a picture of the picture still on the guest's digital camera with her cell phone, and sent the picture to my phone.

As soon as I received the picture, although the quality was not the best (a picture of a picture on a digital camera), I knew there was something special about it. There was no exaggeration; it was a picture of an older woman glaring at me, a woman that definitely was NOT part of the group.

The occurrence became even more eerie when I got to the gift shop later that day. I showed the picture to some of the other tour guides, including the guide that did the tour with me the night before (the crowd was so big we had two guides), who had her group of guests in the basement while I was in the dining room. That night, she told me, there was a considerable amount of activity downstairs, until she said, "Pope is upstairs in the dining room, why don't you go bother him." Evidently whoever, or whatever, was down in the basement did just that.

There have been numerous unusual experiences myself and the other tour guides have experienced in the dining room, including the animatronics playing on their own and the white security chain separating the display and the benches where guests sit moving on its own. But the picture of the mysterious woman glaring at me is one of my favorites, and it hung on my mother's refrigerator until the day she went to be with our Lord and Savior.

CHAPTER 13

OH MY, MISS PEGGY, WHERE'S YOU HEAD?

I am biased, but my daughter is the most loving, caring, kind-hearted, and thoughtful person God ever created. She is the twinkle in my eye, and I could not be prouder of the person she has become. Despite her successes in softball, basketball, and cheerleading, as well as being an honors student, she has always remained down to earth. It is my great honor to be her father.

Growing up, however, I must admit she had one major issue: she was scared to death of everything, including her own shadow. My ex-wife and I divorced when she was about five years old, and she loved spending weekends at my house. The one thing she was not a big fan of was the layout of my house. While she liked having her own bedroom and bathroom, she didn't like that it was at the opposite end of the house from my bedroom. Never wanting to sleep in her own room, I would often wake up in the morning to find her sleeping on the living room couch, which was significantly closer to my bedroom.

I knew better than to allow her to watch any type of horror movie. I made that mistake one time, and she didn't sleep for days. I did not dare take her trick-or-treating until she was ten years old, and even then, she was not too thrilled about it, but she loved the candy.

Every year over Christmas vacation, she and I would spend the week in DuBois, Pennsylvania, with my mother. We always had the best time;

our days were filled with nonstop fun and excitement, but it took years for her to have the courage to sleep in her own room at nanny's house.

She was thirteen years old before she would venture with me into Disney's Haunted Mansion at the Magic Kingdom. When I would take her out to the Sach's Covered Bridge, she refused to walk onto the bridge itself when it was dark. She preferred to sit in the car with the doors locked. I would never venture far from the car when I had her, because I wanted to make sure she was okay.

At eleven years old, her demeanor changed a little bit, and she begged me to take her on one of my tours. At that age I also figured she was ready. After the tour, my ex-wife later informed me my daughter had to sleep in the same bed as her for several days after the tour. My normally happy-go-lucky ex was not happy with me.

The orphanage building, which housed our gift shop, was also home to the Soldier's National Museum. Many people don't know that it also contained two apartments on the upper floors. The owner of our tour company lived in one of the apartments until he passed away, and the other one was rented out. There were repeated unexplained occurrences reported by the renters, including doors opening and closing on their own, lights turning on and off randomly, and sheets and covers being yanked off the beds as its occupants slept. At one point I had the opportunity to rent out one of these apartments, but when my daughter caught wind of my intentions to rent the apartment, she made it clear she would never stay with me as long as I lived there. Choosing my daughter over living in the orphanage was not a difficult decision. She always came first.

Fear is a difficult state of mind to overcome and was a serious problem for her. I felt sorry for her because it held her back at times. Amazingly, this fear did not apply to amusement park rides. She loved the Super Dooper Looper roller coaster at HersheyPark, and we repeatedly rode the ride during the Christmas season when it was about twelve degrees outside. Thankfully, she eventually outgrew the scared-of-everything phase of her life, but not before she spent one extremely long weekend camping with her grandfather in Gettysburg, when she was about 10 years old.

During the Haunted Bus tour, I would share the story of Miss Peggy Noel (No el'). Miss Noel was a resident of Gettysburg who lived and died long before the battle ever took place (yes, Gettysburg did exist before the battle). She was an affluent young woman who met her tragic death on a blustery, snowy night on the way home from a party. Some believe Miss Noel still frequents Gettysburg to this day, particularly in the area she met her demise, looking for what she lost.

When she passed away, winter was in full swing, the days were short, and the temperatures were frigid. There was no Accuweather or super-doppler radar to predict winter storms, which could pop up at any time, lasting for hours or even days. On one of those cold winter nights, Peggy Noel was invited to attend a party in nearby Fairfield. Wanting to attend, she summoned her carriage driver, who hooked up the team of horses.

Arriving at the party, she went inside while her driver remained outside, which was not unusual. A person's social class meant a lot back then, and the driver's place was outside, dutifully waiting for Peggy to return. The driver, however, disobeyed her instructions at least once that evening when he went inside to tell her there was a bad storm happening, and it was time for them to return to Gettysburg.

Peggy was outraged at her driver's disobedience and impropriety of telling her when it was time to leave, so she ordered him back outside to wait. She did not care what his reasoning was, he was nothing more than the hired help. His opinion simply did not matter; they would leave when she was ready.

Several hours passed before the party finally ended. By then, the weather conditions were lousy and travelling was treacherous. When Peggy noticed the hazardous conditions, she wanted to get back to Gettysburg as quickly as possible. She was cold.

During the trip home, the weather conditions continued to deteriorate, as did Peggy Noel's mood. She ordered her driver to speed up as she wanted to get home as soon as possible. Despite his reservations about speeding the horses up, he obliged. Traveling at such an unsafe speed during a snowstorm was leading straight toward disaster, and it did not take long to meet it head on.

Going around a corner, the carriage driver lost control of the team, sending the buggy flipping, ejecting Peggy. The driver regained his composure just in time to see his boss sprawled out on the snow-covered ground, and one of the buggy's heavy wheels bearing down on her. Whether he was horrified at what he saw next or felt vindicated is still a mystery, but he witnessed the wheel crush Peggy's neck, decapitating her and sending her head into the Marsh Creek, causing the driver to scream out "O My Miss Peggy, Where's You Head." Her head was never found.

Whenever I went to the Gettysburg Campground to tell ghost stories, I would follow up the Peggy Noel story with the story about a family of four who were staying at the campground. It is important to know the campground is next to Marsh Creek, at the precise location of Peggy's tragic accident all those years before.

One morning while the family was camping, the mother woke up before anyone else in the camper. It was such a beautiful morning with the sun shining bright and the birds chirping away, she decided to go for a walk. As she was enjoying her early morning stroll along the creek, she noticed something peculiar. She saw what appeared to be a woman standing in the creek, with her back toward the mother. The woman was also bent over at the waist, with her head in the water, and was wearing a vintage-style dress.

The closer she got to the mysterious woman, the more concerned she became. The woman still had not stood up. Was she in distress? The mother was so troubled, she started calling out to her, but received no response. It was like the woman was in her own world, oblivious to anything around her, including another person desperately trying to get her attention.

When the mother was as close as she was going to get without wading into the creek, the woman finally stood up, and when she did, she scared the mother so badly, she let out a scream so loud it reverberated throughout the otherwise quiet camping resort. The woman in the creek had no head! Was it Miss Peggy Noel, still looking for her head?

My family loved staying at the charming Gettysburg Campground. The owners and staff always made me feel at home. If you are looking for a quaint, comfortable place to stay in Gettysburg, I strongly suggest checking this resort first. It is also home to many other paranormal occurrences beyond Peggy Noel.

My father and stepmother stayed at the campground several times a year, and during one of those stays they invited my daughter to join them, which she gladly accepted. They always picked a campsite bordering the creek, which was where they were on that weekend.

I had the absolute pleasure of telling ghost stories by a campfire for my father, stepmother, daughter, and all the other campers. Among the stories I told was the story about Peggy Noel, as well as the story about the family of four whose mother witnessed a headless woman in the creek. In retrospect, telling those two stories while in the presence of my daughter was not the best idea I ever had.

Not only did she not sleep the entire weekend, but during the day she would sit in the lawn chair for hours staring into the creek. When my father asked her why she was staring, she replied, "I'm looking for that woman's head." She was not afraid of the damn snakes hanging from the trees, but she was terrified of seeing Peggy Noel's head. Go figure. To say the least, my father was not too thrilled with my decision to share those two stories.

One final tidbit of information regarding Peggy Noel. The story of her tragic demise is part of the Legends and Showcase inside the gift shop in the orphanage. During the presentation, listen carefully to the voice that calls out, "Oh my, Miss Peggy, where's you head?" That voice should sound very familiar to those of you who participated in any of my tours throughout the years. You guessed it, that voice is me.

CHAPTER 14

GIRL OR WOMAN, YOU DECIDE

The Jennie Wade House on South Baltimore Street has witnessed so much during its existence. When the battle arrived in Gettysburg, the home was only twenty-one years old, and the horror it would see those first three days of July 1863 would be more than enough to destroy any other structure, but it survived.

The house, like Jennie Wade, was spirited, strong-willed, and fearless. The north side of the dwelling is riddled with over one hundred fifty bullet holes, including one through the door, which caused Jennie's death. It also endured a Parrott shell which remained lodged in one of the walls for over fifteen years. Most notably, however, it played host to the tragic events of the morning of July 3, 1863.

The Wade's and McClellan's were not the only family to be in danger and suffer heartache during the Battle of Gettysburg. The widow Catharine McClain, who lost her husband during a battle in Virginia shortly before the engagement in Gettysburg, and her four children lived in the south side of the house. They were forced to leave the comforts of their own living quarters on July 2, 1863 and flee to their cellar after the aforementioned ten-pound Parrott shell ripped through the roof of the McClellan's side, continued through the wall that separated the two sides of the house, and ended up lodged in the brick wall on the McClain side. Many historians believe this was a precursor of the tragedy to happen the following day because the Parrott shell caused Jennie to faint from fear, anxiety, and even exhaustion less than twenty-four hours before her death.

Following Jennie's death, the rest of the Wade and McClellan family, who were still occupying the north side of the battered home, joined Catharine McClain and her four children, who were already nestled away in the cellar.

It is impossible to describe what those unfortunate people went through in that cellar for over twenty-four hours, just waiting for the battle to end and the horror to leave town. Ten people, including Mary Wade; eight-year-old Harry Wade; six-year-old Isaac Brinkerhoff; Georgia McClellan and her six-day old infant, Louis; and Catharine McClain and her four children were stuck in that small area, in total darkness, with the battle raging all around them. A beloved family member's dead body lay just feet away from them, while they not only grieved, but also feared for their own lives. I am sure the question, "Am I next?" crossed their minds more than once. Thankfully, they were not.

During my tours, I felt it necessary to talk about the McClain's. They lived in the home Jennie was killed in, and suffered right along with her family, albeit to a lesser degree. I made it a point to spend a decent amount of time in the south side of the home, including stops in the McClain's second floor bedrooms, kitchen, and parlor.

While on that south side, I would explain how the Union soldiers were able to break through the wall separating the two sides of the home and lead the Wades and McClellan's to safety. I would also tell the sad story of three childhood friends—Jennie Wade, Jack Skelly, and Wesley Culp—who grew up and went to school together. The three had different roles: Jack fighting for the Union, dying from gunshot wounds he sustained prior to the Battle of Gettysburg; Wesley, who had moved to Virginia prior to the start of the Civil War, and subsequently enlisted and fought for the Confederates, and ultimately dying on his own cousin's farm on the third and final day of the battle; and Jennie Wade, the only civilian killed during the battle (approximately thirty minutes prior to Wesley's death). These three young people shared a special friendship and had their entire lives ahead of them, but instead fell victim to the country at war.

While on the McClain side, I would also point out a few of the original items from the house that were present during the battle, including the bloodstained floorboard where Jennie's body laid immediately after she was shot and killed. The ten-pound Parrott shell from the second day of the battle that ended up on the second floor was also on display, and last but certainly not least, the original clock that sat on a mantel on the first floor of the McClain side. I would stress the importance of guests taking pictures of those items and allow ample opportunity for them to do just that.

As a tour guide, I was extremely fortunate that so many guests would share their pictures with me, and with their permission, I would share those incredible photos with future guests.

I received many pictures containing orbs, mist, and shadows, including one absolutely incredible picture of shadow people captured by a husband and wife while we were on the campus of Gettysburg College (which was Pennsylvania College during the battle) during a Friday night bus tour.

One of the first pictures ever emailed to me, which also happens to be one of my favorites, was a picture of the original clock on the McClain's side of the house. The picture was of a female's face and upper body, looking at the clock's glass from the inside. Whenever I would point out the clock during a tour, I would show guests this picture. This prompted guests to snap more pictures, which resulted in me receiving more pictures, which, in turn, resulted in people wanting to see more pictures. While this was a good problem to have, it was still a problem because I could not stand there, in the middle of a tour, showing twenty-five people dozens of pictures. The entire tour would consist of showing pictures, and nothing else.

To appease the growing number of guests who wanted to see the pictures I had in my possession, I introduced the "After Tour Picture Show." I invited everyone who wanted to look at the pictures to stick around after the tour. If they were willing to give up their time, I was willing to do the same.

Using the dusk-to-dawn light in front of the Jennie Wade House gift shop, I would show each picture, explain it, and pass it around so everyone could get a better look. We would engage in conversations about the pictures, with some guests seeing different things than what I saw.

The guests enjoyed the picture review time so much, it became a huge success. Repeat guests told me they could not wait until the tour was over just to see what new pictures I had added to my collection since the last time they were there. It was not unusual for us to spend an hour or more after the tour just to view the pictures.

As mentioned earlier, one of the guest's favorite pictures was the original clock containing the face and upper body of a female. I use the word "female" and not "girl" or "woman" because the picture always produced a spirited, but friendly debate. Is it the face and upper body of a woman or a girl? Some, including myself, think it is the face of a young woman, possibly in her late teens or early twenties, while others are convinced it is that of a preteen or early teenager.

If it is that of a girl, perhaps it is little Susan McClain, who was just two years old during the battle. Being that age, I am sure she could not remember much about her time in the cellar with the Wades and McClellan's on July 3, 1863. Some people (not me) who believe it is a woman, are convinced it is the face of Mary Virginia (Jennie) Wade.

While we will never truly know the age or identity of the face in the clock, it is another example of how I had the most loyal guests a tour guide could ever have. I have received hundreds, if not thousands, of pictures from guests just as enthusiastic now as they were the day they realized they captured something special on their cameras.

The pictures, which I am eternally grateful for, made my five years of doing ghost tours that much better, and I hope it had the same effect on those thousands of guests who stayed with me until the early hours of morning enjoying them, and hopefully many of whom are reading this book right now.

CHAPTER 15

THREE TOURS IN A ROW...
COINCIDENCE OR NOT?

March was always a very exciting month for me. Was it because my birthday is in March? No. Was it because my daughter was born that month? No. Was my yearly review for my full-time job in March? No. It was not Christmas, or Thanksgiving, or the Fourth of July. Finally, March was not the month I was married (that would have produced nightmares, not excitement).

March was exciting because temperatures were starting to warm up. By the Ides of March, the worst of old-man winter was behind us (at least for the most part). The third month of the calendar year also marked the start of a brand-new softball season, as well as my late mother's birthday.

My daughter and I would fly to Florida every March, spending a week with my mother in Weeki Wachee. We would swim with the manatees, relax on a boat ride or two through parts of the Everglades, and take in the breathtaking sunsets over the Gulf.

As an added bonus, March was also the month daylight savings time ended, and we would move the clocks an hour ahead (spring forward), giving us the all-important extra hour of daylight in the evening. What this meant was I would no longer leave my full-time job in the dark.

Last but not least, March was the start of the ghost tour season. Once Halloween had come and gone and Thanksgiving approached, the number of guests taking our tours decreased significantly. With the weather turning cold and the holidays occupying the minds of many, there were nights we struggled to get even one or two guests on our tours. The Saturday after Thanksgiving was our last tour of the season, until the following March.

By the end of November, I was ready for a break; a chance to catch my breath, recharge my batteries, concentrate on basketball, and spend as much time as possible with my daughter. Admittedly, I looked forward to the rest and relaxation that came with the ghost tour off-season, despite the fact I had a very hectic basketball schedule on the horizon.

But the euphoria of having nights and weekends off from the tours only lasted for a couple of weeks. By the start of the New Year, I was missing the tours and the guests tremendously. The adrenaline I felt doing tours was only matched by my days as a member of the prestigious Penn State Blue Band.

Despite the occasional Christmas tour in the Jennie Wade house, or an investigation, or the Saturday night combo tour beginning in mid-January (weather permitting), it just was not the same. We normally had an excellent turnout for these out-of-season tours, but doing ghost tours in January and February was not as exciting, at least where I was concerned. When the season actually started in mid-March, I was more than ready to get back to work.

Kicking off my fourth year of doing tours in 2014, I did an orphanage tour on a frigid weeknight. Unlike the Saturday night combo tours in mid-winter, which did the entire tour inside the building, the March tours followed the normal format of half inside and half outside the building.

That night, by the time we had entered the orphanage, we were all ready to thaw out and enjoy the warmth. As was normally the case, I began the inside portion of the tour in the Legends and Showcase room, and subsequently led the group down the steps, and into the cellar. After leading the guests back down the cellar's hallway and showing them the dungeon, we returned to the main portion of the downstairs.

Much to the delight of the guests, before ending the tour, I turned the lights out for about five minutes. Once the tour ended, and I was driving home, I reflected on my performance. I decided it was a good first tour of the season, except for the bitterly cold.

A couple days after that tour, I received an email from one of the guests. The email explained that while the lights were out in the cellar, her husband felt something scratch his back. He never told anyone, not even her, until they got home. When she looked at his back, she noticed scratch marks. She asked me if I had ever heard of any other guest complaining of being scratched. Answering her honestly, I wrote back that no one had ever mentioned being scratched before.

At the time, I thought perhaps he had unintentionally, and unknowingly, rubbed up against something and got scratched that way. I chalked it up to a coincidence.

Less than a week later, I conducted my second orphanage tour of the young season. The nice thing about the weather in March is one day it can be bone-chillingly cold, like the first tour, and just days later temperatures warm up nicely, as was the case with the second tour. Iin less than a week, guests went from heavy winter coats to a windbreaker.

After that second tour had ended and the guests were leaving, an older gentleman walked up to me and showed me his stomach, which had scratch marks all over it. He explained that something scratched him while the lights were out in the cellar. After seeing the scratch marks and hearing his explanation, my jaw dropped.

Could this have been the power of persuasive thinking at work? A well-known reality television ghost investigator told me, "Since you told the group on the second tour what happened to the husband during the first tour, the gentleman's imagination ran rampant." However, I never mentioned the incident from the first tour to the next tour group. I never posted it on social media, nor did I talk about it with anyone other than the primary principals who were directly involved.

The two guests that were scratched were not related and lived in different states, so the likelihood of the two communicating their experiences to each other was slim. Unlike the scratch marks on the husband from the first tour, I was able to visually see the scratch marks on the gentleman from the second tour. During my ride home, and for the next few days, I kept asking myself if the two incidents were just very strange coincidences.

Three nights later, I was scheduled to do my third orphanage tour of the season. Driving south on Route 15 toward Gettysburg, I pondered what, if anything, was going to happen that night inside the National Homestead at Gettysburg. It would take me most of the night, but eventually that question was answered, and in a big way.

In my two previous years of doing the orphanage tour, I never had anyone tell me they were scratched, so why now? Once again, I decided not to mention a word about what happened to the two previous guests who got scratched. The last thing I wanted to do was scare the handful of children that were taking my tour that night.

The turnout that evening was great, nearly a sell-out, and the guests were enthusiastic. When the tour concluded, I held my breath every time one of the guests approached me, worried someone would say they were scratched. To my relief, nobody mentioned anything. As was customary, a few of the guess had questions, while a few others wanted to get their picture taken, especially with their children.

Since it was a Friday night, we had additional tours that night, so I stayed in Gettysburg to do the introduction for the next tour. Next to the manager, I probably did the most introductions for the other tour guides, and I always liked sticking around our gift shop for a little while on weekends once my tours were over.

Once I finished with the intro, I gathered my bag of ghost hunting equipment, my lantern, and the hat I wore on the tour, and walked across Baltimore Street to my car. Climbing in, I heard people screaming my name. Startled, I looked around, and noticed two guests from the orphanage tour running toward me, frantically waving their hands. What they shared with me sent chills up and down my spine.

After our tour had ended earlier in the evening, the husband and wife walked to the convenience store on the corner of Baltimore Street and Emmitsburg Road, the former location of the Wagon Hotel, renamed the Battlefield Hotel after the battle. During their short walk, the husband told his wife that when the lights were turned out in the cellar, it felt like he had been scratched on his right shoulder blade.

Upon their arrival at the store, the wife looked at her husband's shoulder blade, and noticed scratch marks so deep they had drawn blood. They immediately turned around and ran up the hill, hoping to catch me before I left. Luckily, they saw me climbing into my car and were able to get my attention.

Standing beside my car, he removed his jacked, pulled his right arm out of his sleeve, and, with the light from his wife's cellphone, showed me the scratch marks. To say I was speechless is a massive understatement. I could not believe what I was seeing.

As far as I know, he was the last tour guest to get scratched in the orphanage. But for three tours in a row, the first three of the season, three totally unrelated male guests were scratched. Those three guests did not know each other, and certainly had no knowledge of other guests being scratched. So why did it happen?

We will never know, but I have a few ideas. I think it revolves around Rosa Carmichael. Her reign of terror in the orphanage has been well chronicled, including the mysterious circumstances in which she left Gettysburg. While we do not know what happened to Rosa, it is my belief she continues to make her presence known in the same building which made her infamous.

If it is not Rosa, perhaps it is her task master, a boy by the name of Richard Hutchinson. According to *Webster's New World Dictionary and Thesaurus, Second Edition,* a taskmaster is "one who assigns tasks to others, especially when severe." At that time, Richard was an older boy of nineteen, and should not have been living at the orphanage. It is believed Rosa blackmailed the older boy into overseeing the younger children, assigning them abject, menial, and demeaning tasks, while also physically abusing them.

It also could have been the little boy who, for whatever reason, was heinously and barbarically locked inside an outhouse one Christmas Eve. Thankfully the boy was finally discovered when a neighbor of the orphanage heard his screams and cries. One can only imagine what it was like for that scared little boy. He was undoubtedly freezing cold, scared to death. He was most likely clawing and scratching at the door, trying to free himself.

Another possibility is it was one of the orphans simply playing just a little too rough, but in no way meaning anyone harm. Maybe the child was bored and lonely during the winter break in which they were not allowed outside, so they saw nobody and just got a little carried away.

Finally, it is a possibility the scratching of the three different guests was a mere coincidence; a product of some wild imaginations. Searching for the answer still has me "scratching" my head. What is your theory?

CHAPTER 16

A, B, C . . . 1, 2, 3

As mentioned previously, the primary purpose of the National Homestead at Gettysburg was to take care of the unfortunate children whose fathers died while fighting so bravely and valiantly for others' freedom. The Homestead was to protect the children, feed them, clothe them, provide shelter, and equally important, educate them. These children were young and vulnerable when they were ripped away from the only homes they knew, so providing them with an education also provided them with hope for their future.

If it was not for the much-deserved opportunities afforded them by the formation of the orphanage, children like Eddie Brown, Americus Mitchell, and Frank Humiston would never have had the chance to not only find their identity, but also flourish in a world that had already dealt them a blow in their young lives.

Eddie Brown from New York, one of five siblings whose father was a sharpshooter, had not even reached his fifth birthday when he arrived at the Homestead. He and his siblings would have undoubtedly been lost in obscurity if it was not for the education they received from caring individuals such as Philinda Humiston. As it turned out, while Eddie had a streak of friskiness and prankishness to him, he was a very bright and intelligent young man.

Americus Mitchell, unlike his younger brother, had a physical disability when he first stepped foot into the orphanage and walked with a severe limp. Courageously, he never allowed it to hold him back especially when it came to his studies, where he excelled.

Last but not least was Frank Humiston, the oldest son of Amos Humiston. As noted in chapters 4 and 5, Amos was the soldier who died on the first day of the battle, and was the inspirational force behind the formation of the orphanage. Frank came to the Homestead with his mother, who was the inaugural matron, and his two siblings. The education Frank gained while at the orphanage laid the foundations for success.

Frank attended Dartmouth College after his days in the orphanage, and subsequently graduated from the University of Pennsylvania School of Medicine. Wanting to make a difference by helping others, Frank became a doctor, opened a highly successful medical practice in the state of New Hampshire, and was a wonderful husband and adoring father to his five children.

Academics at the orphanage thrived in the mid to late 1860s and early 1870s under the tutelage of Mrs. Humiston. Knowing education was crucial in the futures of the children she kept, she took pride in her teaching, including preparing them for college, much like she did with her oldest son.

Unfortunately, the high standards of the children's education did not last long. With Philinda's marriage and subsequent departure, priorities quickly changed. Not only did Rosa Carmichael's arrival bring abuse, torture, and neglect, she also de-emphasized academics. The same teachers that put their hearts and souls into teaching the children were either forced to leave, or their total disdain for their new boss caused them to leave voluntarily. Education became an afterthought, which was another contributing factor to the closing of the Homestead. Education was something the children coveted and enjoyed, but was cruelly ripped away from them by Rosa Carmichael.

During a hot, sunny, mid-summer Sunday, I took my daughter, stepdaughter, and one of my stepdaughter's friends, for a day of fun and excitement. Our first stop was an oversized, inflatable waterslide. It was a nice escape from the heat for them.

After leaving the waterslide, I took the girls to Gettysburg and drove them around the battlefield. They climbed around the rocks at Devils Den and hiked up Big Roundtop. The four of us scaled the Pennsylvania Monument, where we were able to overlook the gorgeous Gettysburg countryside, and also walked on historic Sach's Covered Bridge. We took pictures from the top of the castle on Little Round Top, and I explained the story behind the Peace Light Memorial during our stop there. We had a great time in Gettysburg, the girls wanted to see more, and I would have been thrilled to show them, but darkness was setting in and I had a tour to conduct that night.

Begging and pleading to go on my ghost tour, I finally acquiesced. I was hesitant at first for one major reason: it was a tour of the orphanage, which I always considered the most intense tour I conducted, especially for children. The only other time I tried taking my daughter on the orphanage tour, she cried hysterically and had to wait in our gift shop until the tour concluded. I knew, however, waiting in the gift shop this time would not be an option because the shop would be closed long before the tour ended.

The three of them convinced me she would be okay. I explained to my daughter that leaving the tour early this time was not an option, and after her guarantee she would not cry, I agreed to allow them to come on the tour.

As was normal, we began the sold-out tour with the outside portion. There was nothing out of the ordinary, and the three girls were on their best behavior. My stepdaughter's friend had been carrying a backpack around containing windbreakers in case any of them got cold. The backpack also had a notebook, which served as her diary, and a couple of other small items. The backpack itself was pink and gray, and was her normal backpack she used for school.

The moment we entered the orphanage, the K2 meter my stepdaughter's friend was carrying lit up. The activity on the meter signaled possible paranormal activity, and it definitely raised some concerns for her, but she insisted on continuing to carry it.

What she did not want to carry any longer was the pink and gray backpack, so before we headed down into the cellar for the final portion of the tour, she asked me if it was okay if she left it upstairs. Knowing we were the last tour in the building that night, and our gift shop was closed,

I told her to sit it up against the wall between the door leading into the Legends and Showcase room and the bathroom door.

At that time, we still entered and exited the orphanage through the Soldier's National Museum gift shop, which was full of valuable merchandise; therefore, as tour guides, we were required to wait upstairs until all the guests were in the cellar, and be the first one up the steps once the tour was over. As the group started down the steps, I watched my stepdaughter's friend place the backpack exactly where I told her to. Once the backpack was placed, I followed the three girls down into the cellar.

The cellar portion of the tour, everyone's favorite, was more active than usual. The K2 meter continued lighting up, and we even got some reaction using the dowsing rods. It was a fantastic tour, and I was proud of my daughter and the two other girls for the way they conducted themselves.

Ascending the steps first, I was surprised when I noticed the girls were not right behind me. They were more into the tour than I thought they would be. At the top of the steps, I handed out my business cards to the guests who wanted them and thanked them for taking the tour.

As the girls finally made their way up the steps and out of the cellar, the first words out of my stepdaughter's friend's mouth were, "Why did you move my backpack?"

I had not touched her backpack and was shocked when I looked down to where she pointed. The backpack was approximately six to eight feet from where she originally put it, in the corner adjacent to the cellar door.

Looking at each other in disbelief, I explained to the girls I had not moved the backpack, and it took quite a bit of convincing before they finally believed me. The truth is I never touched the backpack and did not give it a second thought until my stepdaughter's friend pointed it out.

Was it a coincidence the K2 meter was active the entire time we were in the orphanage? Was it possible one of the other tour guides used their key to gain entry into the building and, as a practical joke while we were still downstairs, moved the backpack? If that was the case, nobody took credit for it.

While backpacks were obviously not part of the education equation during the orphanage era, children back then, just like today, were curious. It is my belief one or more of the orphans saw the seemingly happy, giggly girls who were about their same age, carrying around something they were not accustomed to seeing, and decided to check it out.

One last oddity about the backpack that night, as the three girls and I were looking in amusement at it leaning at a significant angle against the wall, it had defied gravity by falling backwards. By that time, the girls were more than ready to leave the orphanage. That was the one and only time my daughter cried during that tour. As an aside, the three girls refused to sleep that night without the lights being on.

CHAPTER 17

WHO IN THE HELL IS UP THERE?

An extremely important part of the story of Jennie Wade is what transpired immediately after the twenty-year-old was tragically shot and killed in the kitchen of her sister's home. Yes, the family mourned for their beloved Jennie, but with the relentless bullets still bombarding the home, they had to be concerned with their own survival.

During my Jennie Wade house tours, I always made it a point to emphasize the trek taken by the Wades and McClellan's to the safe confines of the south cellar of the home.

Jennie's mother, who was standing in the kitchen just feet away from her daughter, was the first to realize Jennie was shot and killed. Walking into the parlor where the rest of the family was located, she calmly announced towards her eldest daughter, "Georgia, you sister is dead."

Upon hearing the heart-wrenching news about her younger sister, Georgia bellowed out a blood-curdling scream so loud and terrifying a group of nearby Union soldiers rushed into the home to investigate what had happened, and to make sure the inhabitants were safe. Unfortunately, they quickly learned that not everyone was safe.

After seeing the dead young woman on the floor, the same woman who provided so many of them with food and water, the soldiers had to figure out how to ensure the remainder of the family's safety. Realizing all their lives were in danger, they wanted to get the family out of the crossfire.

They quickly concocted a plan for escape, then had to convince Mrs. Wade she needed to go with them, which was a task easier said than done.

Reluctantly, Mrs. Wade agreed under one condition: whatever the soldiers' plan was, it had to include moving her daughter's body. Mrs. Wade was going nowhere without her. With no time to waste as enemy fire continued to pelt the house, the soldiers agreed.

For obvious reasons, the soldiers knew walking out the door was out of the question. The bullet hole in the door proved that escape route impossible. Instead, they decided their only escape was up the stairs, through the wall separating the two sides of the house, down the south side stairs, out the door (facing friendly fire), and down into the cellar. The soldiers knew if they could get the family down into the cellar, the chances of survival for the remaining living family members would significantly increase.

Carefully escorting the family while also carrying Jennie's body up the stairs, the soldiers utilized the hole in the wall that separated the two sides of the home made by the errant ten-pound Parrott shell that ripped through the home the previous day.

After chipping away at the hole to enlarge it, it was time for the family, including Jennie's corpse, to pass through to the McClain's side. It must have been a horrific scene on the second floor on that sizzling hot early July morning. At one point, Georgia had to hand her infant son off while she crawled through the opening. Mrs. Wade was forced to watch her youngest daughter's body being pushed through the wall, while still having the yeast from bread caked on her lifeless hands. What was the heart-broken matriarch thinking? Did she harbor underserved guilt for not being able to protect her daughter?

There must have been a feeling of doubt in the humid air that tragedy and death was not done for the day. The walls continued to rattle every time a bullet struck the house. What did six-year-old Isaac Brinkerhoff think as he had to be lifted through the opening because he had a physical disability and could not crawl through by himself. Keep in mind he had just witnessed his beloved caregiver killed in front of his eyes.

As the family made it through to the McClain's side, what was Mrs. McClain, who was already in the cellar with her family, thinking when she heard the footsteps above, in her own home? Was it being commandeered by the Confederates? Was her family in danger? Suddenly and without warning, the cellar door flies open, and to her temporary relief, it was the McClellan's and Wades, only to realize tragedy had struck when she noticed Jennie's dead body being brought down the steps.

Movement through the house on that particular day was not done yet after the McClellan's and Wades settled in the cellar. Mrs. Wade, despite having to deal with the death of her daughter, bravely and unselfishly went back up through the home, and back into the kitchen where tragedy had struck just a short time before. Why did she risk her own life going back into the home? She wanted to continue baking bread for the hungry soldiers. How awkward it must have been for her using the same dough Jennie had prepared. She would have been constantly reminded of the horror that had taken place every time she looked to the floor and saw the bloodstained floorboards where her beloved daughter's body had fallen.

After baking the bread, Mrs. Wade went back through the home one last time in order to join the others in the cellar, where they prayed together and waited for the battle to end, which finally occurred a little over twenty-four hours later.

From the beginning of the tour season up until Memorial Day weekend, we would normally only have one tour per night during the week, rotating between the Jennie Wade House and orphanage tours. Even doing one tour a night, there were times the groups were small in number. Schools were still in session and family vacations had not yet begun. It was a peaceful and serene time in Gettysburg, especially if one enjoyed smaller crowds.

I had a mid-week Jennie Wade tour early in the season, and it was a small group of about a dozen guests. I enjoyed the smaller groups for two reasons. First, there was more space for the guests to walk around and take pictures, and second, it afforded me more of an opportunity to interact with the guests on a one-on-one basis. And the guests enjoyed the smaller groups as well.

After concluding the outside portion of the tour, we entered the home, and as usual, I led them through the house, room by room, emphasizing the importance of each room, highlighting and describing the route the family took on that early morning of July 3, 1863.

When we arrived in the cellar, I began my presentation, detailing what happened in that particular area for over twenty-four hours and describing the conditions the inhabitants most likely had to endure. During the early stages of my cellar presentation, I started hearing what sounded like footsteps on the first floor above. Old houses like the Jennie Wade house tend to creak and settle, so I went about the tour without paying too much attention to the strange noises, thinking they would simply go away.

The footsteps did not go away; in fact they intensified, but I never mentioned what I was hearing to the guests. Eventually, however, I noticed some of the guests looking up at the ceiling. This signaled to me they were hearing exactly what I was hearing, but I still kept it to myself.

The footsteps continued, and after a couple more minutes, one of the guests asked me if there was someone walking around upstairs. I explained that we were the only tour that evening, and there had better not be someone else in the house. That explanation seemed to satisfy the guest, at least for the time-being, but failed to satisfy me. Regardless, I continued with my presentation, while thinking to myself, *Who in the hell was upstairs?*

"There's definitely someone up there," one of the other guests announced. It sounded to me like there were several people meandering around upstairs.

As the footsteps continued, I decided to check it out. If somebody was upstairs walking around, I would have to chase them out. Normally, I was very careful about making sure all the doors were locked, but nobody's perfect, so I thought perhaps I forgot this time. All I knew was someone was up there walking around.

Asking if anyone was interested in going back up the steps with me, about half of the guests raised their hands. While the other half of guests remained in the cellar, the other guests and I went on a search-and-expel mission.

Expecting one or more of the doors to be unlocked, I was surprised when they were all secured. We walked through the entire house, room by room, looking under beds and in every nook and cranny of the house, but found no one. If somebody had been walking around, they were gone by that point. Before returning to the cellar, I double-checked one more time that all the doors were locked.

According to the half dozen guests that had remained in the cellar, they heard us walking around and talking, but nothing else. Perhaps whoever was up there heard us coming and ran out. Whatever the case, they were gone, and the tour continued.

There was a problem, however. The footsteps started right back up again almost immediately. Exchanging quizzical glances with the guests, I chalked it up to an unexplainable happening, and finished the tour shortly thereafter, with twelve very spirited guests.

Prior to engaging in the after-tour picture show, I asked a few of the guests to walk back through the house with me one last time, which I always did. Walking back through, we noticed nothing extraordinary, and the doors were, in fact, all locked.

I wonder if the McClain's were as startled as my guests were when they heard the mysterious footsteps coming from above?

CHAPTER 18

THE PROTECTOR

My maternal grandfather, Richard D. Holtry, was an amazing man with an incredibly storied life. He was a jovial man who loved the NFL, *M.A.S.H.*, and the Nightly News. He owned a gas station for decades, gave back to the community he loved, and served proudly during World War II.

After graduating from high school, he enlisted in the US Air Force. Quickly rising to the rank of Sergeant, he saw active duty in World War II.

While participating in a search-and-rescue mission over the South Pacific, my grandfather, who was a top turret gunner on a B-25 Mitchell bomber, was among several airmen who had to eject themselves out of the plane while it was crashing into the ocean. The bomber had mechanical issues and crashed as a direct result of a malfunction with the gasoline pump transferring fuel to the engine.

After surviving the ejection, my grandfather and the rest of the crew were forced to float in a life raft for nearly twenty-four hours until they were rescued just miles from enemy territory, the Japanese shoreline. One of the things my grandfather remembered the most about that mission, and subsequent ejection into the sea, was that dolphins protected the entire crew from the sharks who circled the life raft, trying to get to their next meal.

My grandfather's post-military life was spent operating the Mobile gas station he and my grandmother owned. My grandparents had two daughters and four grandchildren, including yours truly. He was well respected in the community for his unselfish contributions to the local fire and police departments.

In 1988, he was blessed with his first great grandchild, my first niece, Tiffany. His love and adoration for her was obvious from the very beginning. Not only did he sit in a rocking chair for hours rocking her back and forth, but he did it with a smile on his face. Incredibly, Tiffany seemed as enamored with him as he did with her.

Sadly, when Tiffany was just two years old, my grandfather passed away suddenly with a massive heart attack. We lost a beloved family member, and the country lost a true American hero.

While he passed away on Friday, August 24, 1990, it is believed he still makes his presence known to this day, especially when it comes to his great granddaughter. If you ask her, she will tell you he absolutely watches over her, and from some of the stories she told me, along with a firsthand experience or two I witnessed, I agree with her.

Being barely two years old when her great grandfather died, Tiffany had no recollection of what he looked like, but yet an unexplained incident occurred when she was five years old that immediately linked the two together.

Tiffany and her younger sister, Jennifer, who shared the same bedroom, went to bed one night. Shortly after falling asleep, she awoke, and walked toward the bedroom door. To her shock, she noticed a man in full military uniform standing in between the doorway.

Startled, she screamed out for her father, but unfortunately by the time he reached her room, the man had completely disappeared. Sleep was nearly impossible for her the rest of the night because she just could not get the image of the man out of her head.

Eating breakfast, the following morning, she described the man that she saw to her father. Without hesitation, her father had a good idea who she was talking about. Up until that morning she had never seen a picture of her great grandfather, but when my brother showed her a picture of a man in full military uniform, she knew right away it was the same man she saw the night before, her great grandfather, Richard D. Holtry.

As time progressed, her great grandfather continued to make his presence known to her. It seemed to be residual, meaning it happened over and over again but there was really no pattern to it; it did not happen every day, week, or even year, but it continued to happen when she least expected it, especially when the possibility of danger was present in her life.

As she got older and matured, she had a heart-to-heart talk with her great grandfather, explaining that while she appreciated his presence, it did frighten her when he appeared in full body form, like he did that night when she was five. She asked him to please refrain from scaring her like that, and to this day, he has never again manifested himself in full body form. The personal experiences, however, have not stopped.

Her second experience happened when she and her then-boyfriend were in his dorm room at college one night. The dorm room was set up with a bed, desk, and closet. Two people shared each room, and when her boyfriend's roommate decided to go home for the weekend, Tiffany and her boyfriend decided to spend the weekend together in his room. When his roommate left, he gave Tiffany his key, so between her and her boyfriend, they had the only two keys.

When they laid down and went to sleep that night, everything was fine, but when they woke up the following morning, his desk chair was turned at an angle as if someone had been sitting there watching them while they slept. It was angled to a point they could not get out of bed until the chair was moved. They both agreed the chair was not like that when they went to bed the night before. Was it her great grandfather watching over her, making sure she was okay?

The third incident she shared with me happened several years later when Tiffany was living with her then boyfriend. Sadly, that boyfriend was mean and aggressive toward her. Her son also lived with them in the same apartment. As most parents do, she kept the door to their bedroom open so she could hear her son who was in the room across the hall.

At night after her boyfriend returned home, he would lay down in their bedroom. Quite often their bedroom door slammed shut, and she would immediately smell a scent of Old Spice (her great grandfather's favorite cologne). It was her belief that she was being watched over, and even protected from her abusive boyfriend.

It was at this same time period that she was having so many unexplained happenings that she asked me to come to her apartment while her boyfriend was away, bring my ghost hunting equipment, and do an investigation to see if anyone, or anything, was there.

Two statements were recorded on my digital recorder that day that neither of us will ever forget. I specifically asked, "Papaw (the name we both used to call him), are you hear right now?" As clear as possible, the word "yes" was recorded. I also asked, "Is there anything you want to say to her?" and the words "I love you" were recorded. It reduced both of us to tears.

One final series of events occurred when she lived with her fiancé (her son's father) in a mobile home. She would constantly hear noises in the living room and dining room, but never back in the hallway or bedrooms. The noises became so frequent and nerve-wracking, she once again asked me to conduct an investigation, which Alexis and I were more than happy to perform.

Our investigation revealed what seemed to be an unfriendly spirit in the front portion of the mobile home (the living room and dining room). It was our belief that Tiffany's great grandfather was with her in the back portion of the home (again giving off the strong aroma of Old Spice), and whatever was in the front part was scared to venture down the hallway.

My niece is now happily married to a good man who treats her the way a man should treat a woman, so the paranormal encounters have decreased significantly. She still does, from time to time, get that strong whiff of Old Spice, presumably Papaw letting her know he is still around, and still loves her as much as the day she was born.

THE CONCLUSION

A FOND FAREWELL

*I see trees of green, red roses too, I see them
bloom, for me and you, and I think to myself,
what a wonderful world.*

Since moving to Gettysburg, I have been blessed to experience many of the wonderful pleasures life has to offer. The countless beautiful trees I see filled with abundant green around Recreation Park in the middle of July are second only to the exquisite red roses from the United Lutheran Seminary on Buford Avenue to the crazy mess known as the Gettysburg square. The residents in Gettysburg, especially along Buford, take pride in their flower gardens, and while I may sound conceited, I truly believe they were planted for me and you, so we can see them bloom.

*I see skies of blue, and clouds of white,
the bright blessed days, the dark sacred nights,
and I think to myself, what a wonderful world.*

The splendor of the skies of blue, and clouds of white, can be seen all year long, even when the guests of Gettysburg have long returned home. Just the other day, on a cool, brisk October morning, I sat on my balcony, and simply took in the calm serenity of my surroundings, including those never-ending blue skies and angelic, puffy white clouds.

Bright blessed days are what the million or so guests that visit Gettysburg every year yearn for, and Mother Nature rarely disappoints.

What a scene it is when that same bright, blessed day transforms into the dark sacred night. The peacefulness of the quaint, little town can be heard for miles (if that makes any sense), and is a far cry from those first three days of July, 1863. Oh, what a wonderful world it is.

> *The colors of the rainbow, so pretty in the sky,*
> *are also on the faces of people going by.*
> *I see friends shaking hands, saying*
> *"How do you do?" They're really saying "I love you."*

Oh, the colors of the rainbow! I remember driving to the gift shop early one evening. I drove right through one of those brief-but-very-powerful mid-summer thunderstorms. When I looked into the sky, what I saw was breathtaking. I immediately pulled my car over on Route 15 South just to take a picture of the most stunning rainbow I had ever seen. Amazingly enough, the sheer beauty of that rainbow radiated into the streets and sidewalks of the town I love so much, and the harmony exchanged by people walking by was magic. I swear I heard an "I love you" or two resonating amongst the guests. It was truly amazing.

> *I hear babies cry, I watch them grow, they'll*
> *learn much more, than I'll ever know, and I*
> *think to myself, what a wonderful world. Yes,*
> *I think to myself, what a wonderful world.*

Gettysburg and its ambiance are for all ages. The history of this magnificent town is important for both the young and old to know. There were so many guests on my tours who did, indeed, bring their little ones, the future of our world. I was fortunate to watch them grow during my five years.

Joel going from high school in New York to college in Gettysburg. Kennedy from the shy, quiet young lady to the star in her school's musical. I could never forget about Tony, who fought so hard for a normal life, and his ultimate victory, nor Charles' daughter and son, who went from pure terror of our buildings, to staunch supporters of my tours.

Yes, I am privileged to have been able to watch them grow, and am proud to say they have learned much more than I'll ever know. As I say all of this while reminiscing, I am thinking to myself, what a wonderful world. Yes, I think to myself, what a wonderful world! Thank you, Louis Daniel Armstrong, for this song so beautifully written and performed.